There Is Room at the Inn

There Is Room at the Inn

INNS AND B&BS FOR WHEELERS AND SLOW WALKERS

Candy B. Harrington

PHOTOGRAPHS BY CHARLES PANNELL

Demos Medical Publishing LLC
386 Park Avenue South, Suite 301
New York, NY 10016

Cover photograph by Charles Pannell.

Library of Congress Cataloging-in-Publication Data
Harrington, Candy.
    There is room at the inn : inns and B&Bs for wheelers and slow walkers /
Candy B. Harrington ; photographs by Charles Pannell. — 1st ed.
       p.   cm.
    Includes bibliographical references.
    ISBN 1-932603-61-1
    1. Bed and breakfast accommodations—United States.   2. People with
disabilities—Travel.   I. Title.
TX907.2H37   2006
917.306'4—dc22

                                                              2005031590

Manufactured in the United State of America.

06 07 08 09 10   5 4 3 2 1

To Charles

ACKNOWLEDGMENTS

As with all access-related projects, this book was made possible thanks to the efforts of hundreds of people who gave me a hand along the way. Although I truly appreciate all the help, I'd like to offer a very special word of thanks to the following folks.

To Tracey, who first introduced me to bed-and-breakfasts and to the idea that they might actually be accessible.

To Bonnie for her friendship and support, and for her willingness to share information and resources.

To all the innkeepers who have properties listed in this book. They are listed because they took the time to talk with me about the access features of their properties, and because they didn't run away when I mentioned the word "wheelchair."

To all the public relations people and *Emerging Horizons* readers who recommended a property to me. Some of the suggestions worked out and some didn't, but I truly appreciate all of the leads.

To Diana for encouraging me to pursue this idea.

To PB for making me laugh, when I found myself with too many inns and too little time.

And most important, to Charles, for his continued support, his great photographs, and for planting the idea for this book in my head. And for nurturing that idea and living through the creative process with me.

Contents

Preface

My interest in accessible inns and B&Bs began with *Emerging Horizons*. In the early days of the magazine I was always on the lookout for new and creative ways to cover accessible travel. To be honest, some ideas worked better than others.

During that initial creative frenzy I met Tracey Campbell, the then-CEO of InnSeekers. Something clicked between us and she persuaded me to include a column about accessible inns and B&Bs in the magazine. Soon, the InnSider was born. And it grew to be the most popular column in *Emerging Horizons*.

That's the public relations version of the story. Beneath that whole facade there were some serious doubts on my part. To begin with, when I first met Tracey I had never actually seen an accessible inn or B&B. To be quite frank, I thought she was nuts.

Shortly thereafter I heard about an accessible B&B that was just an hour or so from my home. My curiosity was piqued, so I went for a visit. I was amazed. It was accessible. In fact it was very accessible, more so than some hotels I'd seen. I thought about if for a minute or two and then decided to give Tracey the benefit of the doubt. Maybe she wasn't a wacko after all. I decided to give the accessible inn and B&B column a shot.

And the InnSider was a rip-roaring success.

Tracey was the original InnSider columnist, and in those early days it was a learning experience for all concerned. I knew nothing about inns and B&Bs and Tracey knew very little about access. But we both learned. Eventually Tracey went back to her broadcast journalist roots, but the InnSider lived on.

The continued popularity of the subject inspired me to write this book. Over the years, I've spent a lot of time researching accessible inns and B&Bs, and I couldn't include them all in *Emerging Horizons*. There just wasn't enough space. My database of accessible inns and B&Bs grew and grew. After penning a few successful articles for mainstream newspapers about accessible inns and B&Bs, I knew I had to write this book. People were really interested in the subject, and I had all the data.

After all, when you really think about it, inns and B&Bs are a natural choice for people who need accessible accommodations. Why?

- Innkeepers are quick to point out their access shortcomings to prospective guests. After all, if they get something wrong, they have to face the music (and the guest) and explain the error face-to-face.

- Innkeepers know every detail about their property; from the wallpaper pattern in the dining room to the toilet height in the accessible room. And if they don't know something offhand (like the bed height) they can easily go measure it.

- Innkeepers can (and do) block accessible rooms—or any room for that matter—upon reservation. After all, that is how they do business; they assign each guest a specific room when they make their reservation.

Of course, there is a lot more to access than just ramps and roll-in showers. Attitudinal access is just as important as physical access. To that end, this book also contains comments from innkeepers regarding their own attitudes about access. These comments will help you get a real feel for the personality of the individual properties (and the innkeepers).

Additionally, I've omitted properties whose innkeepers demonstrated a bad attitude about access or disability issues. They just don't belong in this book. I interviewed over 700 innkeepers, and to be honest some just didn't pass muster in the attitude department.

For example, one innkeeper who recently added an accessible room to his inventory told me that he didn't want to advertise access in his brochure or on his website because he "didn't want to scare off his normal guests." His property was not included in this book, for obvious reasons.

Then there were the innkeepers who complained about the cost of their access improvements. They talked at length about how much they went in debt and how they will never be able to recover financially. They complained that they were "forced" to include access features in their property and that "disabled people get everything." Those properties were not included either. Again, for obvious reasons.

The bottom line is, the properties listed in this book welcome all guests. Attitudinal access is just as important as physical access.

So how did I find these accessible properties? To be honest, it was a combination of personal experience, on-site visits, innkeeper interviews and recommendations by other travelers. And in some cases it was just plain dumb luck!

I tried to include a good cross section of property types. Of course you'll find the typical New England inn and the down-home B&B in this book; but you'll also find a safari park, a dude ranch, and even some small lodges.

I also tried to get a good sampling of properties from across the U.S.; but to be honest, some locales are just better suited for B&Bs than others. Take this one little mom-and-pop B&B I found (literally) in the middle of nowhere. Now, it had great access, but it seemed like there was nothing to do in the general vicinity. Fearing I missed something, I asked the innkeeper, "Why do people come here?" "Well," he replied, "mostly it's because they break down and they need a place to stay while Hank fixes their car."

Now I realize some people like more activity than others while on holiday, but by the same token I don't really consider "waiting for your car to be repaired" to be a legitimate vacation-time activity. I've done it before, but I've tried to block it from my memory. In any case, I did not include that property in the book. More important, I learned to look to innkeepers for guidance about accessible activities in their local areas. In most cases they provided a wealth of knowledge. And I passed their suggestions along in this book.

And last, but certainly not least, there is the physical access issue. I certainly recognize that even among wheelchair-users, there is a wide range of access preferences. Add slow walkers to the equation and that range dramatically increases. In short, what is accessible to one person may not even be useable to the next.

So how did I determine the minimum access criteria required for inclusion in this book? My basic requirement was that a person in a wheelchair should be able to get in the front door, get in the guest room and use the bathroom. That said, I also realize that there are myriad bathroom preferences. With that in mind, some properties in this book have tub/shower combinations, some have roll-in showers, and some even have low-step showers that can accommodate a shower chair. As in *Emerging Horizons*, the emphasis here is on describing the access so that readers can make appropriate choices.

Diversity aside, I did have to reject some otherwise accessible properties because of a lack of bathroom access. For example, there was one property that had a nicely accessible room, but the bathroom had a claw foot tub. The owner swore up and down that his friend (who is a quad) used it and loved it. That may be true, but I don't think he used the bathtub. It was too high for any type of a shower bench, and there was just no way to transfer. Even somebody who could walk a few steps would have a hard time because of the tub height. And, of course there were no grab bars. That one still stymies me!

Consider this book a starting place; a volume filled with truly unique accessible lodging possibilities. That said, it's important to note that you should always contact prospective lodging choices directly to make sure their access will work for you. It's just a good practice.

When we first introduced the InnSider, accessible inns and B&Bs were few and far between. Happily that is not the case today. With new access laws, an aging population, and a new awareness about access, more and more properties are adding accessible rooms. I'm always on the lookout for accessible inns and B&Bs, so if you stumble across one that I've overlooked, I'd love to hear from you.

Happy travels!

Candy B. Harrington

P.O. Box 278
Ripon, CA 95366
candy@EmergingHorizons.com

Tips for Finding an Accessible Inn

Of course, this book doesn't list every accessible inn and B&B. More and more properties are opening up every day, so it pays to be able to find them for yourself. Admittedly, it can be quite a challenge to track them down. And after you find them, you have to determine if their definition of "accessible" will work for you. All in all it's a lot of work, but the results can be quite gratifying.

So where do you look for accessible inns and B&Bs? Well, love it or hate it, the Internet is the best place to begin your search. Most innkeepers are quite adept at using the Internet for promotional and marketing purposes, so that's where you'll find the most updated information.

A simple search on "inns" and "wheelchair" will yield some interesting results. Although many inn websites don't include any access information at all, some at least note if their property is wheelchair-accessible. This can mean a variety of things, so further research is necessary in order to determine the true level of accessibility. Still, it's a starting point.

Although there are many internet-based inn and B&B directories, only a few give any meaningful access information. Innseekers (innseekers.com) was the first web directory to address access. Although specific access details are not listed for the properties, you can search this directory for accessible inns.

Bed & Breakfast Inns Online (bbonline.com) is a newcomer to the access arena; however, it's showing a lot of promise. As with Innseekers you can search for accessible properties on this website, and in some cases access details are also included. I say "in some cases," because it's incumbent upon the innkeeper to enter the access details. Some properties include detailed access information while others only state that they have an accessible room. Basically, it's a great way to narrow down your search.

One of the most important things to remember when searching for inns is to always inquire about access, even if you don't think there's any chance that the property could be accessible. While researching this book, I found that many innkeepers failed to mention their access in any of their promotional materials. In most cases this was an oversight; however, if I had not asked a few key questions, I would have passed up some great properties. Even if there happens to be a flight of 20 stairs leading to the front porch, don't discount the possibility that another entrance may be accessible. Always ask about access. You may be surprised at the answers you receive.

It goes without saying that you have to ask some detailed questions about access. How many questions you ask will depend on your access needs. For example, if the exact placement of grab bars is important to you, then you really need to ask for measurements. Although most properties have grab bars, their placement is not always standard.

Never overlook the obvious. For example, one time I asked the innkeeper to describe the accessible room in detail. It sounded great, but when I arrived there were 10 steps up to the front porch and no accessible entry. They had an "accessible" room but no way to get there.

What questions do you need to ask? Well here's a copy of my access checklist. I used it to screen properties and narrow down my choices. Granted, you may need to personalize it for your specific needs, but it hits the major access areas. It's a good starting point, and a great way to get in the habit of asking the right questions.

Access Checklist

1. Entry

Is your main entrance accessible?

Is it ramped?

Is it a level entry?

Are there steps? If so, how many?

Do you have a portable ramp?

Do you have an alternative accessible entry?

If so, where is it located?

Is it ramped?

Is it a level entry?

Are there steps? If so, how many?

Do you have a portable ramp?

2. Parking

Do you have accessible parking on your property?

If so, how close is it to the accessible entrance?

3. Pathway

Do you have more than one floor?

If so, is there elevator access to all floors?

On what floor is your accessible room located?

4. Accessible Guest Rooms

What is the name or room number of your accessible guest room?

Is the doorway clearance at least 32 inches on all doors (including interior doors)? If not, please note narrower clearances.

How high is the bed? This is especially important to ask at Victorian inns, which may have very high beds.

Do you have an open-frame bed?

Do you have a roll-in shower?

If no, what type of bathing facility do you have?

If yes, does the shower have a level (flush) threshold?

Do you have a shower seat or bench available?

If so, what kind?

Do you have a hand-held shower?

Are there grab bars in the shower?

Are there grab bars around the toilet? (If specific grab-bar height and placement are essential for your transfer, be sure to ask about exact measurements.)

How high is the toilet?

Does the bathroom have a roll-under sink?

5. Public Rooms

Are the doorways to all of your public rooms at least 32 inches wide?

Do your public rooms have any steps or other access obstacles?

Does your breakfast room have barrier-free access?

If not, do you offer breakfast delivery to the room or other alternative arrangements?

Are there level paths to your outdoor areas?

6. Other

Do you have a floor plan of the accessible room available?

Do you know if there is an access guide for your area?

Do you have any special access features or programs that you would like to mention?

A Few Notes for Innkeepers

Undoubtedly when some innkeepers read this book they will wonder why their property isn't included. They will probably say something like, "My inn is just as accessible as Joe's, and his is listed but mine isn't. Why?" Well, there's a good answer to that question, and I think it's very important for innkeepers as a group to understand that answer.

In fact, by understanding that answer, it's my hope that more innkeepers will truly realize what is missing (access-wise) from their own property. It may be something very easy to fix, and fixing it may make their property more attractive to wheelchair-users and slow walkers. And when I go searching for properties for the second edition of this book, their property may strike my fancy.

It's not that I intentionally omitted properties from this book—to be honest, those that were not included were not included for one of four very simple reasons.

1. I didn't know about the property.
2. The access just wasn't there.
3. The innkeeper could not answer my access questions.
4. The innkeeper had a bad attitude.

I DIDN'T KNOW ABOUT THE PROPERTY

You can build the most accessible property in the world, but if you don't tell people about your access features, or even the fact that your property is wheelchair-accessible, your efforts are wasted. Some of the properties I included in this book I came across because of recommendations from other travelers; yet when I went to the property website, nary a word was mentioned about access.

I can only assume that there are many more properties that I didn't include that suffered from the same problem. Access should be noted on the home page, and that's very easy to do with the international symbol of accessibility. The same symbol should also be included in print materials.

Of course many innkeepers think that noting access is unnecessary. "After all," said one innkeeper, "everything has to be accessible today because of the ADA." Of course we know that's not true, and in many cases inns and B&Bs are exempt from access regulations. That's why access should be prominently mentioned. The general assumption is that inns and B&Bs are not accessible unless otherwise noted.

THE ACCESS JUST WASN'T THERE

Granted this book has a wide range of accessible properties, because different people truly do have different access needs. Some of the properties in this book work great for power wheelchair-users, while others are only appropriate for slow walkers or part time wheelchair-users. It should be noted that although I didn't totally eliminate any property just because it lacked a roll-in shower; there comes a point where you just can't classify some properties as accessible in any way, shape or form. Unfortunately I reached that point more than a few times, and in most cases the innkeepers were clueless.

The most common access problem I encountered was the entrance, and I don't mean a two-inch threshold either. I was truly amazed at how many properties had 12 to15 stairs at the entrance, with no alternate entry, yet the innkeepers still insisted their inn was accessible. When I pointed out the problem, their comeback was the standard, "Well we have had people in wheelchairs here before, but they could walk up stairs," or (my personal favorite) "As long as they bring somebody to carry them up the stairs, our inn is 100% accessible."

Although accessible means different things to different people, I don't think anybody truly defines it as "being carried up 15 stairs." To be fair, many innkeepers just aren't used to seeing wheelchair-users, and they think that everybody in a wheelchair can get up and walk. I tried to emphasize the fact that carrying people is not the norm; yet whenever I did, I usually got the reply of, "Well, Norma uses a wheelchair and she doesn't mind being carried. She can walk, too." When the conversation got down to that level, I usually just thanked the innkeepers for their time and moved on to my next property.

THE INNKEEPER COULD NOT ANSWER MY ACCESS QUESTIONS

Admittedly my initial screening questions were somewhat cumbersome; but to be honest I fully expected detailed answers from the innkeepers. The questions I asked were not unlike the questions that prospective guests would ask, so if the innkeepers didn't have the time (or the inclination) to answer my questions, it's doubtful they would treat prospective guests any better. Communication is essential where access is concerned.

On the positive side, most of the innkeepers I contacted were happy to field my questions; however, sometimes their answers were less than complete. For example, I would ask if the accessible guest room had a roll-in shower, only to receive the pat reply, "Everything at our inn is ADA-compliant." In short, the innkeeper did not answer my question, or even attempt to answer it. I also have to add that I found 28-inch doorways at some of those inns that claimed to be "ADA compliant." Obviously those properties are not included in this book.

The point is, the term "ADA-compliant" is meaningless to the average traveler. After all, just because you use a wheelchair doesn't mean you know the access codes. You know what works for you, and that is why you need to ask questions—to see if the property meets your specific access needs. Two properties located right next door to each another can have entirely different access features, yet both can still be termed "ADA-compliant." Asking questions is essential, and innkeepers need to take the time to fully answer them. Those that didn't are not included in this book.

THE INNKEEPER HAD A BAD ATTITUDE

Finally, I ran into a few innkeepers that just had a bad attitude. To be honest, I think a few of them forgot that they are in the hospitality business.

A few innkeepers went on and on about how much their access modifications cost and how they didn't feel they should have to make their property accessible. "After all," said one innkeeper, "those people don't travel that much anyway. It's just a waste of my money."

Obviously those properties were not included, because attitudinal access is just as important as physical access. The good news is, I found plenty of innkeepers with good attitudes, so I didn't even need to worry about the ones with the bad attitudes.

In the end, I really enjoy finding new accessible properties, and I look forward to finding even more for the next edition of the book. So if you think your property has what it takes to make the cut, drop me an e-mail. I look forward to hearing from you. Really!

There Is Room at the Inn

Camai B&B

ANCHORAGE, ALASKA

According to innkeeper Caroline Valentine, Camai B&B is "Anchorage's oldest and most frequently remodeled B&B." Located in a quiet residential area about 20 minutes from the airport, Camai B&B has three suites, including the accessible Fireweed Suite.

As Caroline tells the story, the Fireweed Suite was originally designed for her mother-in-law. Says Caroline, "Craig's mother has since told us that she is too busy traveling and that she doesn't like the cold winters up here. So that's how our accessible room was born."

The ground-floor Fireweed Suite has a private entrance with ramped access from the nearby driveway. The entry has a level threshold, and the suite features a queen-sized bed, a private bath, a kitchenette, and a sitting room. The bathroom has a tub/shower combination with a hand-held shower and a portable bath bench. There are grab bars in the shower area and around the toilet, and there is a roll-under sink in the bathroom.

The kitchenette includes a sink, microwave, refrigerator, coffeemaker and a toaster. Says Caroline, "Since the Fireweed Suite has a kitchenette, I serve breakfast there when I have guests who are wheelchair-users. I serve a full breakfast (with a gourmet touch) in the summer, and an expanded continental breakfast in the winter."

Nightly rates for the Fireweed Suite range from $75 in the winter to $125 in the summer. And Caroline adds, "There are discounts for consecutive-night stays."

Anchorage is a great place to enjoy the outdoors; in fact Chugach State Park just about surrounds the city. There are a number of accessible trails and viewing areas, including Lower Bird Ridge Trail, Bird Point Scenic Overlook and Potter Creek Interpretive Trail.

Lower Bird Ridge Trail is approximately 1/4-mile long and includes a paved pathway and a boardwalk. There are viewing platforms at both ends of the trail, and accessible restrooms at the upper end of the trail. There is no cross slope on the 4.5-foot wide trail, and it's easily maneuvered in a wheelchair. The trail offers an intimate view of a typical South Central Alaska forest with birch, aspen, willow, alder, spruce and cottonwood trees.

Bird Point Scenic Overlook is located at mile 96 of the Seward Highway and includes a wheelchair-accessible walkway with spectacular views of Turnagain Arm and the Kenai Peninsula. And if you're lucky, you might even spot a Beluga whale out feeding near the point.

The half-mile long Potter Creek Interpretive Trail begins as a paved trail, and then turns into a hard-packed dirt trail. It ends at the inaccessible Turnagain Arm Trail, so the round-trip hike is about a mile. There is a spotting scope at the beginning of the trail with great views of Upper Cook Inlet, the Kenai Mountains and the Alaska Range. There is also an overlook in the lower parking area that faces a marshy wildlife habitat. This whole area is prime wildlife habitat for moose, bears, small game and birds. You just never know what you will see.

Of course if you'd rather sit back and relax at Camai B&B, you might just spot some wildlife there too. As Caroline points out, "Moose frequently nibble the flowers in our award-winning garden."

Camai B&B
3838 Westminster Way
Anchorage, AK 99508
(907) 333-2219
www.camaibnb.com

Iditarod House B&B

When Donna and Glen Massay built their dream home in 1997, they planned ahead. As Donna puts it, "We didn't want age to force us to leave our retirement home, so we incorporated a number of access features into the original design. Our home has 36" doors, wide halls, large bathrooms, and a complete bedroom, bath and laundry on the main floor." She adds, "While the entire house is not currently accessible, only minor changes will be necessary (if needed) in the future. So, with that frame of mind, it was easy to do an accessible bath in the B&B, especially since it was new construction."

The 3,500-square-foot Iditarod House B&B is only one mile from downtown Palmer, yet it's located in a pristine wooded area, which offers great views of Pioneer Peak. The 2 ½-story home is set into a hillside so there are really two ground levels; the B&B entrance is in the front and the innkeepers' entrance is in the rear.

There are no steps at the front entrance, but there is a three-inch lip at the front threshold. Says Donna, "I have a four-foot ramp that I put in place whenever it's needed." Accessible parking is available at the end of the paved brick walkway, and a new covered brick patio stretches across the front of the house. Donna notes, "The new patio is a great place to enjoy the view and watch the bird feeder." She adds, "The pea gravel driveway can be problematic for some wheelchair-users, so make sure and park close to the walkway."

The accessible Americana Room has a tub/shower combination with a hand-held shower and a transfer seat. There are grab bars in the tub and toilet areas and a five-foot turning radius in the bathroom. The bathroom also has a roll-under sink.

The ground level Iditarod Room has the same accessible entrance as the Americana Room; and although the bathroom is roomy, it does not have a five-foot turning radius. There are small grab bars in the tub and toilet areas, and Donna notes, "The Iditarod Room has accommodated a person with a walker before."

The Iditarod Room and the Americana Room share a dining area, located on same level. There are no stairs or raised thresholds throughout the common area.

Nightly rooms rates for both the Americana Room and the Iditarod Room are $70 (May 15 to September 30), and $65 during the rest of the year. There is a five-night minimum stay.

Donna also is full of helpful suggestions for accessible activities in the area, and since she is a retired musher, the Iditarod Trail Race Museum tops her list. Donna proudly proclaims, "For twenty years, I raced sled dogs, completing the Iditarod Trail Sled Dog Race twice. In 1980 I placed 10th and in 1981 I placed 18th. Bet you can guess how our B&B got its name!"

The Iditarod Trail Race Museum is wheelchair-accessible and includes a free display of the history of the Iditarod Trail and the sled dog race. During the summer, there are also a sled dog team and puppies on the premises. Other accessible suggestions include the Musk Ox farm, the main viewing area at Matanuska Glacier Park and the accessible trails at Kepler-Bradley State Park.

And Donna adds, "Don't forget the new paved walkways at the Independence Mine at Hatter Pass. It's just a gorgeous area; an alpine tundra above the tree line which looks out over the Matanuska Valley. It's a favorite of many guests."

Iditarod House B&B
12100 Woodstock Drive
Palmer, AK 99645
(907) 745-4348
www.iditarodhouse.com

Feathered Nest B&B

The Feathered Nest B&B is conveniently located just a few blocks from the Alaska Ferry Terminal, in a quiet, family-oriented neighborhood of Petersburg, Alaska. The spacious 900-square foot B&B apartment unit is separated from the innkeepers' residence by a common entry and the laundry room. Says innkeeper Liz Bacom, "The laundry room makes the perfect sound barrier, and it also gives our guests a higher level of privacy."

The apartment has a lot of personal touches; in fact it was originally designed for Liz's mom. Liz explains, "When my mother was diagnosed with ALS we decided to tear down the old two-car detached garage and build an addition that would accommodate her future needs. Sadly, she did not live to see the project completed, but her artistic touches are everywhere!"

The spacious apartment features an open floor plan with plenty of room to wheel around. Although there are two steps up to the front deck, Liz has a portable ramp that she puts in place whenever it's needed. The main entry door is 42" wide, and the doors in the apartment are all 36" wide. There is a small private deck, although it's big enough for a wheelchair.

The kitchen features a roll-under sink and stove; however, the counter tops are standard height. The lower cabinets feature roll-out shelves, and there is a side-by-side refrigerator in the kitchen. Everything is within easy reach. The kitchen is fully stocked, so guests can prepare their own breakfast at their leisure.

The bathroom features a roll-in shower with a hand-held showerhead and a fold-down shower seat. There is a pedestal-style sink with a single lever handle, and there are grab bars in the toilet and shower areas. Liz chuckles, "We have a good friend who is a wheelchair-user and he visits us frequently. He told us he would take the bathroom home with him if he could!"

And last but not least, the bedroom has a very comfortable dual-controlled air bed. Says Liz, "Everyone that has slept on it has loved it."

Winter rates at the Feathered Nest B&B are $75 per night, and summer rates (May 15 to September 15) are \$110 per night double, \$100 per night single. There is a two night minimum stay.

Keep in mind that Petersburg is a small community with a population of about 3,200. The downtown shopping area and the majority of the stores are wheelchair-accessible, but most of the gravel roads are tough going for wheelers. Additionally some of the side streets leading up from the water are quite steep. There is no public transportation in the town, so it's best to drive your own car or van and come over on the ferry.

That said, if you like small towns, you'll love Petersburg. For a real slice of small-town Alaskan life, try to schedule your visit to include one of Petersburg's many annual festivals. Petersburg was settled in the 1890s by Norwegian fisherman, so the major celebration is the Little Norway Festival. It is traditionally held around May 17, which is Norwegian Independence Day.

Other noteworthy events include the Salmon Derby, which is held over Memorial Day weekend, and the week-long August Quilt Camp, which is organized by the Rain County Quilters. Confides Liz, "The Fourth of July is never more fun than in a small town, where everyone who loves a parade can also be in the parade. We even have fireworks, but not until after 11:00 at night."

Feathered Nest B&B
P.O. Box 683
Petersburg, AK 99833
(907) 772-3090
www.featherednestbandb.com

A Taste of Alaska

A Taste of Alaska is situated on 280 secluded acres, just 15 minutes outside of Fairbanks. This 10-room lodge is located on the 1947 homestead site of Walter and Dorothy Eberhardt. The Eberhardts originally developed the land for farming, but the 7,000-square foot lodge was added in 1995. Walter still farms the land today.

The Eberhardts goal was to capture the flavor and taste of Alaska in their lodge. The natural log-cabin structure was constructed from spruce trees that were logged from the homestead, and the interior is decorated with antiques and Alaskan collectibles.

The original structure did not include any accessible rooms, but innkeeper Debbie Eberhardt decided to change that after she chatted with two of her early guests. Recalls Debbie, "The second year in business I met a couple that had to leave their disabled child at home. I felt bad for them, so I told them when I expanded I would include a wing that was wheelchair-accessible." And Debbie followed through on her promise.

Today the West Wing Suite features great access and spectacular views of Mt. McKinley, the Alaska Range, and the Trans-Alaska Pipeline. This spacious suite is located on the upper floor and it has a private entrance with ramp access. The suite is 32' by 24' 6", and it can be configured with one, two, or three queen-sized beds.

The bathroom includes a roll-in shower, a hand-held showerhead and grab bars in the shower and around the toilet. Guests have their choice of two shower chairs. Both the bathroom and the suite have extra-wide double doors that swing outward.

Breakfast is served in the main dining room, which is located next door to the West Wing Suite. Breakfast is served buffet style, but table service is available upon request.

There is also an accessible public bathroom located on the main floor of the lodge. There is ramp access to the main floor entrance, and accessible parking approximately four feet from the main entrance. The driveway area is paved with rocks from Brown's Hill Quarry, and it slopes gently down to the grass. Says Debbie, "We have had guests who use motorized wheelchairs, and they did just fine on both surfaces."

The West Wing Suite rents for $185 per night.

As for accessible attractions in the area, Debbie recommends the Riverboat Discovery, the University of Alaska Fairbanks Museum, and the Fairbanks Ice Museum.

The Riverboat Discovery features historic day cruises on Alaska's inland waterways. There is ramp access to the authentic sternwheeler; and the itinerary includes a stop at an Athabascan fish camp and a Chena Indian village.

The University of Alaska Fairbanks Museum features five galleries that highlight the natural and cultural history of Alaska. And where else but the Fairbanks Ice Museum can you find over 30 tons of ice sculptures?

Of course many people come to Fairbanks to view the aurora borealis. And since A Taste of Alaska is located away from the city lights, it's a great place for stargazing and the ideal spot to enjoy the spectacular Northern Lights.

A Taste of Alaska
551 Eberhardt Road
Fairbanks, AK 99712
(907) 488-7855
www.atasteofalaska.com

Majestic Mountain Inn

PAYSON, ARIZONA

As its name implies, the Majestic Mountain Inn is located in the mountains; but not just any mountains. This 50-room inn lies smack in the middle of scenic Arizona Rim Country, approximately 75 miles northeast of Scottsdale. The drive itself is worth the price of admission.

As you leave the Scottsdale metropolitan area and head towards Payson, you'll notice that the saguaros are soon replaced by ponderosa pines. The towns are few and far between on this stretch of road; and as the elevation increases you begin to feel the stress melt away. As you roll into Payson, you're finally able to breathe deep, unwind, and relax. And as luck would have it, relaxation is the specialty of the house at the Majestic Mountain Inn.

"Comfortable" is the adjective that first comes to mind when I think of the inn. "Accessible" runs a close second. All of the public areas, including the pool, meeting room, and front lobby, offer barrier-free access. Paved level pathways wind through the property, and accessible parking spaces are located directly in front of the accessible rooms. Both of the accessible rooms are located on the ground level, and they each offer a different degree of access.

Room 101 is a standard room. Access features include a level entry, wide doorways and plenty of space to maneuver. The bathroom has a tub/shower combination and there are grab bars in the shower and around the toilet. A refrigerator, coffeemaker and a VCR are standard amenities in all rooms.

Room 119 is a luxury room. It is also the most accessible guest room at the inn. Access features include wide doorways, a level entry, lowered closet rods, and lever handles. The bathroom has a roll-in shower with a hand-held showerhead, grab bars in the shower and around the toilet, and a five-foot turning radius.

This guest room also has a large sitting area with a fireplace, a two-person Jacuzzi tub, and a small back porch that borders a greenbelt. The back door is 36" wide and there is a one-inch threshold out to the patio. There's plenty of room to wheel around in this spacious room.

Room 119 at the Majestic Mountain Inn features a large sitting area and a back porch that borders a greenbelt.

Rates for the standard room range from $62 to $99 per night, and rates for the luxury room range from $89 to $140 per night. The lowest rates are available during the week.

Payson is a good place to beat the heat in the summer and enjoy the scenery all year long. Just 10 miles up the road you'll find the very scenic and accessible Tonto Natural Bridge State Park. Tonto Natural Bridge is 183 feet high and is believed to be the largest natural travertine bridge in the world. An accessible trail leads from the waterfall parking lot to three scenic viewpoints. The trail is paved and offers some great views of the natural bridge and the waterfall.

All in all, the Majestic Mountain Inn is a great place to relax. It's a place where it's easy to stay "just one more day."

Majestic Mountain Inn
602 East Highway 260
Payson, AZ 85541
(928) 474-0185
www.majesticmountaininn.com

Maricopa Manor

PHOENIX, ARIZONA

*L*ocated in the heart of North Central Phoenix, Maricopa Manor takes its name from the Native American tribe that once inhabited the area. Today the property is appropriately billed as "a private oasis in the heart of the sixth-largest city in the U.S." Indeed, the privacy afforded guests at this hacienda-style inn is a very attractive feature. In fact, Maricopa Manor is designed with privacy in mind; you never feel cramped, crowded, or surrounded by other guests, even when there's a full house.

The entire manor consists of two buildings, which are located in a quiet residential neighborhood. The main manor house was built in 1928. This two-story building houses a few guest rooms plus a living room, kitchen, and study. The luxury suites are located next door in the guesthouse build-

The hacienda style design of Maricopa Manor offers guests level access to the buildings, courtyards, and gardens on the property.

ing. Together these buildings share an entire acre of land filled with mature landscaping, accessible garden paths, a pool and a quiet gazebo.

After a number of renovations, the property debuted as a B&B in 1989. Jeff Vadheim, a retired family physician, bought Maricopa Manor in December, 2000. Jeff continued to make renovations, additions, and access upgrades after he took over ownership. He installed an accessible public restroom, enlarged some of the suites and expanded the public areas. Today the inn has two rooms that contain access modifications.

The Victorian Suite, which is located in the manor house, was the residence of the former owner (a wheelchair-user). It's decorated with Victorian antiques and has a queen-sized bed. Access features include wide doorways, grab bars around the bathtub, and limited pathway access through the suite. There is a level entry to the suite through the French doors from the patio. This room is most appropriate for manual wheelchair-users who can walk a few steps to transfer, as there is not a five-foot turning radius in the bathroom.

The most accessible room on the property is the Palo Verde Suite. This spacious two-bedroom suite features a king-sized bed in one bedroom and a three-quarter size spool bed with a trundle in the other bedroom. The bathroom includes a pedestal sink and a low-step shower (bring your own shower chair). Other access features include a level entry, wide doorways and good pathway access. There is a two-inch step inside the suite, but a portable ramp can be installed with advance notice.

Says Jeff, "One guest stayed here for over a month while his own home was undergoing access renovations. He had muscular dystrophy and used a wheelchair. His attendant came to stay with him as well. The Palo Verde Suite worked quite well for him."

The pathway access throughout the grounds is excellent; level sidewalks and no obstructions. Assigned parking is located close to each suite. Breakfast is delivered to your room every morning at a prearranged time. You can choose to dine in your suite in your bathrobe or enjoy your breakfast basket in the garden.

Nightly rates for the Victorian Suite range from $89 to $159. Rates for the Palo Verde Suite range from $99 to $209 per night. The low season runs from June to September.

Accessible sights in the area include the Heard Museum, the Arizona Science Center, the Pueblo Grande Museum, and the Desert Botanical Gardens. Maricopa Manor makes an ideal home base for a Phoenix museum-hopping holiday. Many shops and restaurants are also located nearby.

Jeff continues to make improvements to his property, so check back often to see if he has added any new accessible rooms to his inventory.

Maricopa Manor
15 West Pasadena Avenue
Phoenix, AZ 85013
(602) 274-6302
www.maricopamanor.com

Two Sedona Gems

*L*ocated in Northern Arizona, Sedona is famous for the spectacular red rock formations that virtually surround this mountain community. Some call it a museum without walls, others think of it as a spiritual retreat, and still others consider it more of an artists' haven. The bottom line is, no matter how you describe it, Sedona is well worth a visit.

Because of its somewhat remote location, Sedona is best done as a driving trip. In fact, many people couple it with a visit to the nearby Grand Canyon. And although there are a few large chain properties in Sedona, it's always nice to stay at a smaller property that actually captures the local flavor. Two Sedona properties jump to the head of the list in that respect: the Southwest Inn and the Lodge at Sedona. Both are noted not only for their above-average amenities, but also for their accessibility.

The Southwest Inn features 28 rooms, all with private decks and fireplaces. This Santa Fe–style property is 100% non-smoking and has two accessible rooms.

Rooms 115 and 120 are both located on the ground floor and they each have a level entry, wide doorways, good pathway access, and a king-sized bed. The bathrooms each have a tub/shower combination with a shower bench and a hand-held shower. There are grab bars in the toilet and tub areas, and there's plenty of room to maneuver in these spacious rooms. The private patios are located near the spa, which also has ramp access.

The public areas, including the pool and lobby, have level or ramped access. Accessible parking is located about 10 feet from the lobby door.

The only public space that lacks access is the breakfast area; however, innkeeper Sheila Gilgoff says, " We are happy to deliver breakfast upon request, since the breakfast area is not accessible." And what could be better than enjoying breakfast on your own patio with a view of Sedona's red rocks?

Rates for the Southwest Inn range from $99 to $219 per night.

The Lodge at Sedona is billed as a Frank Lloyd Wright–inspired property that marries Mission-style artistry with inviting warmth. This 14-room

The Meadow Breeze Suite at the Lodge at Sedona offers
good access and plenty of room to maneuver a wheelchair.

luxury inn is situated on three beautifully landscaped acres and is surrounded by red rock vistas.

The accessible Meadow Breeze Suite is located on the ground floor of the main building. There are two entries to this room, the most accessible one being the front entrance, which has level access through the main lobby. There is also ramped access to the room from a private back deck; however, the pathway leading up from the back parking lot has many steps. Still, the deck is a great place to relax and enjoy a glass of wine and watch the sunset. Accessible parking is located near the front lobby entrance.

This spacious suite features a king-sized bed, a fireplace, and a two-person (not accessible) Jacuzzi tub. The Continental-style bathroom features a roll-in shower with a hand-held showerhead, grab bars in the toilet and shower areas, and a raised toilet.

There is plenty of room to maneuver throughout the suite, but some people may have trouble accessing the bed, which is located in a half alcove. The top half (the area near the head of the bed) only has 26 inches of clearance on each side; but the bottom half (near the foot) has a full 36 inches on both sides. Although some wheelchairs can squeeze in this space and access the bed, the innkeeper is quite willing to move the bed to accommodate larger (and even standard-size) wheelchairs. Don't be afraid to ask if you have problems.

There is barrier-free access to all the very comfortable public rooms at the Lodge at Sedona. Breakfast is a full five-course gourmet affair, and it can be served in the dining room or out on the deck. I recommend the deck if the weather is nice.

And as an added bonus, innkeeper Shelley Wachal is very knowledgeable about the area attractions and she is happy to make sightseeing suggestions and help you with your plans. A large number of maps and sightseeing brochures are available in the main lobby.

The nightly rate for the Meadow Breeze Suite is $275.

Of course the most popular thing to do in Sedona is to enjoy the great scenery. Two ways to do this are on a jeep tour or aboard the Verde Canyon Railroad.

Although none of the local jeep tours have roll-on access, Red Rock Jeep tours can accommodate some wheelchair-users. You have to be able to transfer to the front seat in order to take the tour, but the guides are happy to assist with transfers. The ride gets a bit bumpy but the scenery is spectacular. Granted this is not an option for everybody, but for the most part the folks at Red Rock Jeep Tours are willing to do what they can to make things accessible. Stop by and talk with them and see if this tour is an appropriate choice for you.

The Verde Canyon Railroad, which is billed as "Arizona's longest-running nature show" is a very accessible option. This four-hour narrated train tour departs from nearby Clarkdale and offers accessible boarding and seating for wheelchair-users.

Accessible parking is located close to the station, and there is lift access to the train. Wheelchair-users can opt to stay in their own wheelchairs or transfer to a train seat during the ride. There are some width limitations, but loaner wheelchairs are available if your wheelchair exceeds the 25-inch maximum width. Says Assistant Manager Robyn Breen, "We do what we can to make things work. Sometimes we even have to take the batteries off of power wheelchairs because they are too heavy for the lift. The lift can accommodate up to 300 pounds."

All in all, it's a very accessible way to explore red rock country. The bottom line is, they take good care of you aboard the Verde Canyon Railroad, and the employees do whatever they can to make your trip more pleasant.

Southwest Inn
3250 West Highway 89A
Sedona, AZ 86336
(928) 282-3344
www.swinn.com

Lodge at Sedona
125 Kallof Place
Sedona, AZ 86336
(928) 204-1942
www.LODGEatSEDONA.com

Country Charm B&B

BISMARK, ARKANSAS

*I*nnkeeper Jerry Allensworth recalls, "I retired from Caterpillar in 1999, and we moved to Arkansas to build a house and get out of the rat race." That retirement house ultimately became an inn when the Country Charm B&B opened its doors in 2000. Back then it only had one guest room, but Jerry continued his expansion over the years. Today the inn has four guest rooms, including one that is wheelchair-accessible.

Innkeeping seemed a natural retirement choice for Jerry and his wife Mari. As Jerry puts it, "We are both very good with people. We can read them and put them at ease quickly. This is the perfect business for us and we know it."

The Country Charm B&B is located in Bismark, which is a small bedroom community outside the Hot Springs area. Says Jerry, "We built the inn at the back corner of a 20-acre parcel. We could have put it in front by the highway, but we like to enjoy our 20 acres every time we drive in and out."

Jerry added the wheelchair-accessible Garden Level Suite in 2003. He recalls his motivation. "The Vice President of the Bed and Breakfast Association of Arkansas is a double amputee," says Jerry. "She stayed with us a couple of times and told us that we were very close to being accessible already. She made suggestions, so I took a couple of extra steps to make things accessible. It opened up a whole new market to us."

The lower-level Garden Level Suite features a level entry with easy access to the private parking area. The bathroom has a tub/shower combination, a shower seat and a hand-held shower. There is plenty of room to maneuver around the suite, and access to the covered deck is just off the main dining room. There is a three-inch step and a 36" door out to the deck.

The deck is 11' above ground level. The house is built into the side of a hill so the main floor is at ground level in the front, while the lower floor is at ground level in the back. Says Jerry, "Everything can be accessed easily by anyone. Since we only have four rooms, I'm able to help anyone that needs assistance."

Other inn amenities include a stocked fishing pond located just a "stone's throw away" from the covered patio. Jerry adds, "I also bait hooks and remove fish for those who are squeamish." A six-foot-wide nature trail winds through the adjacent woods. This .8-mile trail is maintained with a lawnmower in the summer, and the first part of the trail is slightly uphill. Again, Jerry points out that he is able to assist guests who may have trouble accessing the first part of the trail.

The Garden Level Suite rents for $125 per night.

Jerry looks forward to sharing the joys of country living with all of his guests. Says Jerry, "We like the country because we don't hear sirens, busses or late night pedestrian traffic. The noises we like are hoot owls, whippoorwills, and our rooster clearing his throat at dawn. We see deer from our covered back deck and have ducks swimming on our pond. What could be better?"

Country Charm B&B
8354 Highway 84
Bismarck, AR 71929
(501) 865-1842
www.bbonline.com/ar/charm

Lookout Point
Lakeside Inn

HOT SPRINGS, ARKANSAS

*S*ometimes you can tell a lot from a name. Take Lookout Point Lakeside Inn for example. With a name like that, you'd expect to find an inn on a lake with some great views. And you won't be disappointed, because that's exactly what it offers. Located on beautiful Lake Hamilton in central Arkansas, this 10-room inn features great scenery, comfortable rooms, superb lake views, and two very hospitable innkeepers.

Innkeepers Ray and Kristie Rosset moved to Hot Springs from the Dallas area in 2001. After two years of hard work, they welcomed their first guest to the inn on February 14, 2003.

The Rossets made it a point to include some barrier-free features in their new home. "We intentionally set out to create a B&B that is friendly to all persons," says Kristie. "Besides," she adds, "Clara Jean (a friend of ours who uses a wheelchair) would have our hides if we didn't include a place of welcome for her!"

Each of the Rossets' guest rooms is named after a small Arkansas town. Quips Kristie, "You should see the list of towns that we rejected!" The barrier-free room is named Calico Rock, and it is located on the first floor. There is level access to the first floor, and the accessible parking area is adjacent to the entry. The sun room, sitting room, library, and dining room are also located on the first floor.

The Calico Rock Room has a queen-sized iron bed plus a twin bed. Says Kristie, "We avoided the super-sized mattresses in this room, opting for ease in maneuvering from wheelchair to bed." The bathroom features a large roll-in shower with a hand-held showerhead and a built-in shower seat. There are grab bars in the shower and around the toilet, and there is adequate space to maneuver in both the bathroom and the bedroom. And the best thing about this room is the view. As Kristie puts it, "The lake view from this room is awesome."

The Calico Rock Room also has a private terrace with barrier-free access to a garden path. The path crosses the creek, passes by a waterfall, and winds down to the lakeside. With the help of a landscape architect, the Rossets designed the pathway to meet the grade criteria for accessible design.

Nightly rates for the Calico Rock Room range from $150 to $165.

And there's certainly no shortage of accessible attractions in the area. Nearby Hot Springs National Park is the nation's oldest designated National Park site. And downtown Hot Springs features historic Bathhouse Row, a national museum, plus an operating bathhouse with thermal mineral baths and massages. Kristie recommends visiting the promenade behind Bathhouse Row. "It is a lovely, accessible walk," she says.

And don't miss the downtown gallery walk on the first Friday of the month. As Kristie points out, Hot Springs is fast becoming a booming fine arts community.

"There's really plenty to do here," says Kristie. "So come on down and relax, feast and play."

Lookout Point Lakeside Inn
104 Lookout Circle
Hot Springs, AR 71913
(501) 525-6155
www.lookoutpointinn.com

Music Express Inn

CHICO, CALIFORNIA

*I*t goes without saying that the nine-room Music Express Inn is nicely accessible; after all, one of the owners is a wheelchair-user. Says innkeeper Irene Cobeen, "My husband Barney is the chef and he does all of the cooking from his wheelchair. He's a great cook and he can prepare a hearty breakfast or whip up something lighter—whatever you choose."

Besides making their own inn accessible, the Cobeens encourage other innkeepers to do the same. "We sat on an industry panel at the Professional Association of Innkeepers International conference in Reston, Virginia," says Irene. "We talked about things you could do to your inn to make it more comfortable for wheelchair-users. I'd like to see more innkeepers make the effort, as it's not really that hard."

As for their own property, the Music Express Inn has good pathway access throughout the house and ramp access at the front doorway. Because there is a wheelchair-user living here, you can rest assured there won't be any furniture blocking your way. There is a gravel parking lot in front of the accessible Fall Room, but you can also park on the pavement in front of the main house.

The first-floor Fall Room has two full-size beds and features wide doorways and a very accessible floor plan. There is a refrigerator and a microwave conveniently located at wheelchair height, and the room has a great view of the wedding garden.

The bathroom features a full five-foot turning radius and a roll-in shower with a hand-held showerhead and a portable shower bench. Other access features include grab bars in the shower and around the toilet, and a pedestal sink.

The public rooms, including the first-floor rehearsal hall, meeting room, and dining room all feature barrier-free access.

Nightly rates for the Fall Room range from $61 to $125.

"We are a university and agriculture community," says Irene. "Bidwell Park is the second-largest park in the U.S., and it's very accessible. They have a lot of trails there and they just opened a new observatory, which is accessible. Many events, like 'Shakespeare in the Park' are also accessible. And because bicycling is so popular here, we also have a lot of trails that are wheelchair-friendly. It's really a pretty good town for wheelers."

Music Express Inn
1145 El Monte Avenue
Chico, CA 95928
(530) 891-9833
www.northvalley.net/musicexpress

Garnett Creek Inn

CALISTOGA, CALIFORNIA

This Northern California inn is housed in a Victorian home that is over 125 years old. In May 2001 it was acquired by the present owners, who restored and remodeled it. Today this quaint five-room inn is located near the center of town, within walking distance of a number of restaurants, shops and spas. It's a great choice for a romantic weekend or a midweek getaway.

Since the property was remodeled in 2001, certain access features were required as a matter of code. Of course, since one of the owners has muscular dystrophy and uses a wheelchair, they went a little beyond code as far as access modifications are concerned. They wanted to make sure their inn was accessible to everybody. In the end, they did a very good job.

The inn features lift access from the street to the porch, with accessible parking located just a few feet from the lift. The Fair Isle Room has level access from the porch and is furnished with a queen-sized bed and a gas fireplace. Access features include wide doorways, good pathway access and lowered environmental controls.

The bathroom has a roll-in shower with a hand-held showerhead and a fold-down shower seat, grab bars in the shower and around the toilet, and a roll-under sink.

All of the public areas are accessible, including the living room, sitting room and front porch. There is a brick walkway through the garden that provides good access to most of the garden area.

Breakfast is generally delivered to the room; however, innkeeper Marlys notes that other arrangements can be made. "Many of our guests prefer to enjoy their breakfast on the front porch," she says. "It's a very pleasant place to linger over your meal."

Nightly room rates range from $185 to $235. The highest rates are on Friday and Saturday nights.

Although many people come to Calistoga to kick back and relax, there are also a number interesting diversions in the neighborhood. "Visiting Wineries is the big attraction in the Calistoga area," says Marlys. "Also, the Old Faithful Geyser and the Petrified Forest are accessible. Spa treatments and mud baths are also very popular."

Garnett Creek Inn
1139 Lincoln Avenue
Calistoga, CA 94515
(707) 942-9797
www.garnetcreekinn.com

Fallon Hotel

COLUMBIA, CALIFORNIA

*O*riginally constructed as a brick boarding house in 1859, Columbia's Fallon Hotel has definitely stood the test of time. Over the years it escaped fire and destruction as it operated under a variety of names including the Kress Hotel, the Columbia Hotel and Opera House, the Smith Hotel, and the Columbia Inn. In 1986 this aging property was restored and renamed for Owen Fallon, the man who built the original structure. Today this historic 14-room inn is operated by the Columbia City Hotel Cooperation, and enthusiastically managed by innkeeper Tom Bender.

Tom has a great love of Columbia history and he can usually be found dressed in period clothing, sharing historic tidbits with visitors. Says Tom regarding the renovation of the Fallon House, "While we tried to remain as faithful to 19th-century decor as possible, modern conveniences such as indoor plumbing, heating and air conditioning were added for the comfort of our guests." Another modern convenience added during the renovation was a wheelchair-accessible guest room.

The Fallon Hotel features level access, a wide entry door and plenty of room to maneuver a wheelchair in the lobby. Accessible parking is available in a nearby city lot, as vehicle traffic is not permitted in this historic town.

The accessible room (14) is located on the ground floor and features wide doorways and good pathway access, and it is the only guest room with a full bathroom. Access features in the bathroom include a roll-in shower with a fold-down shower bench and a hand-held showerhead, grab bars in the shower and around the toilet, and a roll-under sink. It's simple but very nicely done.

All of the public areas, including the adjacent ice cream parlor (where breakfast is served) feature barrier-free access.

The nightly rate for Room 14 is $80.

Columbia is the perfect place for history buffs, as it exists pretty much as it did during the California gold rush. A stagecoach roars through

Room 14 at the Fallon Hotel includes a bathroom with a roll-in shower.

town on a regular basis, children play with their hoops and sticks in front of the blacksmith shop, and Dr. Jhon entertains Main Street visitors with a few tunes.

As far as access goes, some businesses have level access, some have hidden ramps, some have small thresholds, and some have steps. It's really a mixed bag, but there's lots to enjoy even if you can't access every building.

For a real treat, make plans to attend one of the four murder mystery weekends held every January and February. Written and produced by a professional theatrical company, they are great fun, and they include two nights lodging, a Friday night reception, three meals on Saturday, brunch on Sunday, entertainment, taxes, and gratuities. Best of all, according to Tom, "If a wheelchair-user signs up, we make sure all of the murder mystery activities are held in accessible locations."

Fallon Hotel
11175 Washington Street
Columbia, CA 95310
(209) 532-1479
www.cityhotel.com

Romantic Oceanside Retreats

HALF MOON BAY, CALIFORNIA

Many people visit Half Moon Bay to enjoy the spectacular coastline. I have to admit, I'm one of those people; so finding lodging on the beach is a top priority for me. I just love to sleep with the windows open and listen to sound of the surf. Fortunately I didn't have to search too hard on my latest coastal excursion, as the Beach House fit the bill perfectly.

Located next to Surfers' Beach, the Beach House features 54 ocean-front lofts. Access is excellent throughout this luxurious inn, with barrier-free pathways, wide doorways and level thresholds. General Manager Charlie Dyke also gets high marks for both attitude and follow-through in

The Beach House patio is a great place to relax and enjoy the view.

the access department, as he goes to great lengths to make sure all of his guests are comfortable.

The Beach House has four accessible guestrooms, including one (101) with a roll-in shower. All rooms have a separate living and sleeping area, plus a microwave, refrigerator, wet bar and a small cooktop. In short, everything you could possibly want or need for a romantic getaway. There is good pathway access throughout the spacious rooms, with level access to the balcony or porch. The accessible bathrooms all have a five-foot turning radius, a roll-under sink, and grab bars in the shower and around the toilet.

Other access features of the property include ample accessible parking, good pathway access to the lobby, and elevator access to the upper floors. There is also a sling lift available for the oceanfront pool and Jacuzzi. As an added bonus, there is level access to the paved coastside trail next door at Surfers' Beach. It's a great way to enjoy the scenery.

Nightly rates at the Beach House range from $165 to $355.

Another favorite oceanfront property I discovered quite by accident. In fact, I actually won a weekend stay at Landis Shores. It was one of those door-prize giveaways where you just toss your business card in the fish bowl. Apparently Lady Luck was on my side that day, as my card was drawn.

I decided it would be a great place to spend my birthday weekend. My original plan was to take a few days off of work and just get away from it all. Well, that worked fine until I had a gander at the accessible room at Landis Shores. It was just too good to pass up, so I whipped out my notebook and starting jotting down the details. I just had to share this great accessible find.

Landis Shores is billed as a luxury inn, and I have to admit that's an accurate description. This eight-room property is located on romantic Miramar Beach in Half Moon Bay, just 30 minutes south of San Francisco. The property was constructed in 1999, and innkeepers Ken and Ellen Landis built it to be accessible from the ground up.

Access features include accessible parking, a level entry, and elevator access to the second floor. Admittedly the front door (which remains locked) is quite heavy; however, you can always ask for assistance over the intercom. The intercom at the door is connected to the front desk, which is located upstairs and is staffed from 8:30 A.M to 8:30 P.M.. Generally speaking, the staff at Landis Shores is very eager to do whatever they can to make their guests more comfortable, so if the door is a problem for you, be sure and let them know.

The San Francisco Bay Room at Landis Shores features an open-frame queen-sized bed, with adequate pathway access on both sides.

All of the guest rooms and public spaces are located on the second floor. The accessible San Francisco Bay room includes an open frame queen-sized bed, wide doorways, lever handles and extra electrical outlets. The bathroom features a five-foot turning radius and has a roll-in shower with a hand-held showerhead, a roll-under sink, and grab bars in the shower and around the toilet. A portable shower chair with a back is available upon request. The room also has a VCR, a gas fireplace and a private balcony. There is a one-inch lip on the balcony threshold, but it's doable for many people.

There is barrier-free access to all of the upstairs public spaces, including the living room, dining room, public restrooms and VCR library area. Wine and cheese appetizers are served in the living room every afternoon. Breakfast can be served in the dining area or delivered to your room.

The San Francisco Bay Room rents for $285 per night.

And for that romantic dinner, check out the Historic Miramar Beach Restaurant, located right next door. This Prohibition-era roadhouse is now billed as the most romantic restaurant on the coast, and even though it's historic, it has an accessible entrance and parking.

Just up the coast you'll find the Moss Beach Distillery, which has great food and features some dramatic views of Half Moon Bay. There is ramp access to the first floor and elevator access to the basement level. And as an added bonus, the Moss Beach Distillery is rumored to be haunted.

There are several scenic beaches in the Half Moon Bay area. Venice Beach and Francis Beach both have beach wheelchairs for loan at the entry stations. Francis Beach also has an accessible boardwalk that extends into the snowy plover nesting area and connects to the paved coastside trail.

The bottom line is, both of these properties are ideal venues for a romantic weekend getaway. After all, nothing beats the romance of the ocean.

Beach House Inn
4100 North Cabrillo Highway
Half Moon Bay, CA 94019
(650) 712-0220
www.beach-house.com

Landis Shores
211 Mirada Road
Half Moon Bay, CA 94019
(650) 726-6642
www.landisshores.com

Mendocino Picks

MENDOCINO, CALIFORNIA

*I*f the beauty of the rugged California cost appeals to you, then consider a visit to the Mendocino area. Located about 160 miles north of San Francisco, this secluded coastal area offers great ocean views plus the charming historic village of Mendocino. And if you're looking for a romantic getaway, Mendocino is a favorite pick. There are many inns and B&Bs throughout the area, as it's also a popular weekend destination. Properties range from quaint to expansive, and many have accessible rooms. Here are some of my top picks.

The Inn at Schoolhouse Creek is situated on over eight acres and features ocean-view gardens, meadows, and a secluded beach cove. The 15-room inn was purchased several years ago by Steven Musser and Maureen Gilbert, but the former innkeepers, Al and Penny Greenwood, live just down the street.

Al and Penny did the access renovations and added the Thyme Cottage. Says Penny, "Even though we researched extensively as to design requirements, our most valuable suggestions came from a wheelchair-user who is a friend of our carpenter."

The Thyme cottage includes a tiled bath with a tub/shower combination, a hand-held showerhead and a shower seat. There is a five-foot turning radius in the bathroom and grab bars around the toilet. The guest room features a queen-sized bed, a microwave, and a gas fireplace.

An 1862 farmhouse serves as the reception, lobby, and breakfast area. This historic structure is not accessible by the front door, but some wheelchair-users are able to access it through the back entrance which goes through the office and the kitchen. Even this path is pretty narrow and may not be doable for many people. Still, there is another option, as breakfast can always be delivered to your room upon request.

The rate for the Thyme Cottage is $175 per night.

The Brewery Gulch Inn offers a different perspective on the area, as it's perched on a hillside overlooking Smuggler's Cove. The whole inn was constructed from 150-year-old virgin redwood, which was painstakingly salvaged by the owner, Dr. Ciancutti.

The inn opened in 2001, and an accessible room was incorporated into the original design. This first-floor room is simply called Redwood. It features a private deck with an ocean view, a queen-sized bed and mahogany furnishings. The spacious bathroom has a roll-in shower with a hand-held showerhead and a fold-down shower seat. There are grab bars in the shower and around the toilet, and a roll-under sink. Says a recent guest, "My favorite features about the room were the gas fireplace and the deer that appeared at my patio door at 4 A.M."

There is barrier-free access to the first-floor pubic areas, where breakfast and afternoon wine and hors d'oeuvres are served.

Nightly rates for Redwood range from $170 to $200.

The Stanford Inn is billed as a working certified organic garden and farm with an inn. It's also the home of Ravens, one of Mendocino's acclaimed vegetarian restaurants. As innkeeper Joan Stanford puts it, "We attempt to embody healthy living styles."

The 38-room inn sits atop a meadow and is surrounded by forest on the north, east, and south sides and Mendocino Bay on the west side. The Forest and Big River Buildings house the guest rooms and the Ravens Building houses the lobbies and the dining room

When the Stanfords remodeled and added the Ravens Building, they added two accessible rooms. They are known as rooms 200 and 203, but they will probably be given more descriptive names in the future.

During the renovations the former lobby was enlarged and converted to an accessible room. This spacious room has good pathway access and includes a bathroom with a roll-in shower, a hand-held showerhead and a built-in shower bench. There are grab bars in the shower and around the toilet. The old registration parking area was converted to accessible parking and a ramp was added for easy access to the room.

The Stanfords also converted their old side shed into a large, accessible bathroom and then joined it to the existing next-door unit. Says Joan, "This is now one of our largest single units. We were able to take out the original bath and create a more interesting and accessible room."

Breakfast is served in the dining room in the new Ravens Building, which features an accessible entry and barrier-free access throughout. The garden path is paved, but it is too steep for most manual wheelchair-users. Says Joan, "A motorized wheelchair works just fine in the garden, though."

The room rate for the accessible rooms at the Stanford Inn is $265 per night.

I've saved my favorite pick for last: Rosie's Cottage. Located just outside of Mendocino in Little River, this quaint offering has two very accommodating owners. Ron and Rosie really understand access issues and are happy to do whatever they can to make your stay more enjoyable.

Rosie's one-bedroom cottage features French-door access from the bedroom to the garden. There is a futon in the living room, and the cottage also has a fully equipped kitchen. Some of the furniture may need to be moved for optimal pathway access, but Ron and Rosie are happy to oblige.

The bathroom has a low-step shower with a hand-held showerhead. It's important to note that there is a seven-inch lip on the shower. A plastic shower chair with a back is provided. The bathroom also has grab bars around the toilet and a roll-under sink.

Rosie provides the fixings to make your own breakfast, so you can make it in the cottage at your leisure. It's a great getaway place and the perfect site for a romantic rendezvous.

The rates for this undiscovered gem range from $110 to $140 per night.

As far as access in the town of Mendocino goes, it's pretty hilly and the curb-cuts and sidewalks are inconsistent. Still, many of the shops, restaurants, and galleries are accessible. The accessible Mac Callum House restaurant comes highly recommended by many innkeepers. But truly the most popular thing to do in Mendocino is to just relax and admire the views and enjoy the natural beauty.

The Inn at Schoolhouse Creek
7051 North Highway One
Little River, CA 95456
(707) 937-5525
www.schoolhousecreek.com

Brewery Gulch Inn
9401 North Highway One
Mendocino, CA 95460
(707) 937-4752
www.brewerygulchinn.com

The Stanford Inn By The Sea
44850 Comptche Ukiah Road
Mendocino, CA 95460
(707) 937-5615
www.stanfordinn.com

Rosie's Cottage
44635 Little River Airport Road
Little River, CA 95456
(707) 937-5477

Captain's Inn

MOSS LANDING, CALIFORNIA

The Captain's Inn is a unique combination of old and new. This 10-room nautical-themed inn consists of two buildings: the renovated Pacific Coast Steamship Company building and the newly constructed boathouse. And although innkeepers Melanie and Yohn Gideon had to incorporate an accessible guest room into their inn, they had a few choices. It would have been easier to build the accessible room in the new addition; however, they chose to locate it in the historic building.

Says Melanie, "When we were planning our inn, we learned that many historical buildings are not accessible. Many disabled people told us they wished they could stay at historical inns, but they had problems finding accessible properties. So, during our renovation we decided to modify a downstairs room in our historical building and make it accessible."

The accessible First Mate room has wide doorways, level access and a 36-inch clearance on one side of the bed. The spacious bathroom has a full five-foot turning radius, a roll-in shower with a hand-held showerhead and a fold-down shower seat. Other access features include grab bars in the toilet and shower areas and a roll-under sink with a lowered mirror.

The only tight spot in the room is the historic fireplace hearth, which is about two inches high. Because of this obstacle, it's only possible to access one side of the bed in a wheelchair. The TV is located on the far side of the bed, but Melanie can move it over to the accessible side upon request. Still, this room is very nicely done access-wise, and the whole inn has some great creative touches.

The newly constructed boathouse building also has three ground-floor guest rooms that will work for some slow walkers. The Sanctuary, Cast Away, and River Front rooms are located close to the parking lot and feature wide entry doorways and good pathway access. They don't have any grab bars or other bathroom adaptations; but the low-step showers are very spacious, and doable for many people.

It's important to also note that some of the beds in the boathouse rooms are quite high. In fact, these beds are made from boats that were once used in the Monterey area. For example, the bed in the Sanctuary Room is a 38-inch-high marine biologist's dingy and trailer—complete with working tail-lights. It's definitely one-of-a-kind.

Access to the public areas of the inn is excellent, including ramped access to the historic building from the back parking lot. Wide doorways and good pathway access are present throughout the ground floor public areas

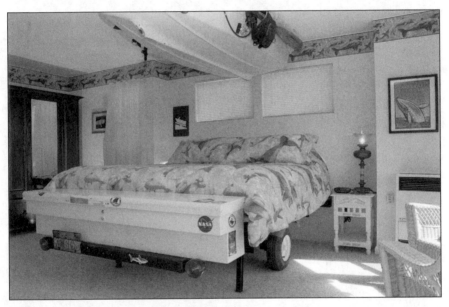

The Sanctuary Room at the Captain's Inn includes a
bed made from a marine biologist's dingy and trailer.

of the historic building. Accessible parking is located between the historic building and the boathouse, with access to both buildings.

The nightly rate for the First Mate room is $135. The boathouse rooms each rent for $195 per night.

Melanie is also the unofficial Moss Landing visitors' information center, and she is happy to help out with sightseeing and dining suggestions. Charlie Moss's, a casual restaurant and bar, is a fun place to go to visit with the locals. It's located right down the street from the Captain's Inn and has accessible parking, a ramped entry, and an accessible men's restroom (which women can also use).

Moss Landing is a great place for nature lovers. A top pick for birders is the barrier-free Upper Slough Trail in nearby Kirby Park. One of the best things about this trail is that it's relatively deserted, even during the peak season.

And for an up-close-and-personal experience with the bay's inhabitants, join Captains Step and Heidi for a whale-watching cruise aboard Sanctuary Cruises' newest vessel, the Princess of Whales. Most wheelchair-users will need some assistance on the floating dock (it's bumpy and the entrance is steep) but the Princess of Whales features roll-on access, and wheelers can roam around the outside deck or opt to transfer to a comfortable seat in the main cabin.

Slow walkers should also check out Elkhorn Slough Safari Tours, a two-hour pontoon boat cruise through the Elkhorn Slough Wildlife Reserve captained by Yohn Gideon. There is a 12-inch step up to the boat, but the crew is happy to offer assistance.

All in all, Moss Landing is the ideal place to relax, get away from it all, and enjoy Mother Nature.

Captain's Inn
8122 Moss Landing Road
Moss Landing, CA 95039
(831) 633-5550
www.captainsinn.com

Victoria Inn

MURPHYS, CALIFORNIA

T he Victoria Inn has a very special place in my heart; after all, it was my first accessible inn. I heard about it from a friend, who claimed it was wheelchair-accessible. Unfortunately this particular friend really didn't have much knowledge about access issues, had never actually seen the inn and in the end was just reporting what she had "heard." Admittedly she wasn't a very reliable source. My curiosity was piqued however; and since Murphys is only about an hour away from my home, I decided to check it out in person. I didn't expect to find much, but I like the drive, especially in the spring. In short, I didn't think I had much to loose.

I was amazed at what I found. In fact, the Victoria Inn is still one the nicest accessible properties I have ever seen. Actually it's the first new inn to be built in historic Murphys in some 136 years, which probably accounts for much of the good access. This 12-room inn takes you back to yesteryear as it's lovingly decorated with antiques, family heirlooms, keepsakes and artwork. You feel like you are in your grandmother's house, only it's accessible.

There is a ramped entry to the front porch and barrier-free access to the public areas on the first floor of the inn. Mae's room is located on the first floor just off the lobby. This spacious room features wide doorways, lever handles, lowered controls and even a lowered closet rod. Access features in the bathroom include a roll-in shower with a hand-held showerhead and a fold-down shower seat. There is a five-foot turning radius in the bathroom, and there are grab bars in the shower and around the toilet.

Besides being accessible, it's also nicely decorated. The bathroom features deep blue tile, wainscoting, wallpaper, and lots of wood trim. Rose, teal, brass, and pine work together to create a cozy atmosphere throughout the rest of the suite. A flowered comforter, dried flower arrangements, and a comfy rocking chair round out the homey decor.

Breakfast is served in the first-floor dining room, which is surrounded by bay windows. There is good pathway access throughout the dining

Mae's Room at the Victoria Inn is an
excellent choice for wheelchair-users.

room, and the wooden floors make wheeling a piece of cake. The adjoining parlor is the site for the wine and hors d'oeuvres reception that is held each evening. All in all, the Redbud Inn is quite a find in this restored California gold rush town.

Mae's Room rents for $95 per night.

The main attraction in Murphys is the ambiance of this historic town. Main Street is lined with boutiques, restaurants and historical shops. Some are accessible and some aren't. The sidewalks in Murphys, like in other historic gold country towns, are not the most accessible. Many are high and lack curb-cuts. Still there are a number of accessible shops and restaurants, but don't go there expecting every business to be accessible. The Victoria Inn is located just off Main Street in the back of the Miners Exchange complex, so there is pretty good access to that shopping area.

Murphys is a fun place to visit, and if you can go in the spring, the wildflowers in the surrounding countryside are simply spectacular. It's one of those places where the scenic drive is a destination by itself.

Victoria Inn
402 Main Street
Murphys, CA 95247
(209) 728-8933
www.victoriainn-murphys.com

Blue Violet Mansion

NAPA, CALIFORNIA

*L*ocated in the heart of Northern California wine country, the Blue Violet Mansion is a beautifully restored 1886 Queen Ann Victorian home. This 17-room inn is set amidst an acre of manicured gardens in Old Town Napa and offers Old World charm, gourmet dining, and all the ingredients for that perfect romantic getaway. And although many historic properties are not accessible, the Blue Violet Mansion was remodeled in 2000 to include a number of access upgrades.

During the remodeling, a new fine dining room was added to this National Register of Historic Places property. Access improvements included a new accessible entrance and improved pathway access on the first floor. At that point the decision was also made to convert the former dining room and the adjoining bathroom to an accessible suite. Thus the accessible Duchess's Parlor (also known as room 9) was born.

The Duchess's Parlor features a gas-burning fireplace with an oak mantel, wooden wainscoting, and a brass king-sized bed that faces the redwood trees in the garden. This spacious room includes a roll-in shower, lowered environmental controls and great pathway access. The old brass bed fits nicely into the room decor; but unlike some of those tall Victorian canopy beds, the mattress height of this model is a more manageable 24 inches. The room is very nicely done, and best of all, the access upgrades were added without detracting from the historic nature of the property.

The public areas of the inn are also nicely accessible with wide hallways and doorways throughout the first floor. Outdoors, both the heated pool and the hot tub are accessible by wide, level concrete sidewalks. Accessible pathways also wind through the Victorian garden, which features a rose garden and a period gazebo.

Nightly rates for the Duchess's Parlor range from $189 to $239. Midweek winter rates can sometimes be a little lower if the inn is running a special promotion.

Innkeepers Bob and Kathleen Morris agree that Napa is best known for its wineries and wine tasting. Many of the area wineries are accessible, and the Wine Train is accessible to manual wheelchair-users who can transfer to a boarding chair. Downtown Napa, Yountville, St. Helena, and Calistoga all offer great shopping. Additionally the area is blessed with a number of excellent restaurants, many of which are accessible.

And reminds Kathleen, "We also have an excellent chef right here. Guests may choose to dine in our beautifully appointed dining room or opt for a more romantic dinner in their own room."

Blue Violet Mansion
443 Brown Street
Napa, CA 94559
(707) 253-2583
www.bluevioletmansion.com

Inn at Occidental

OCCIDENTAL, CALIFORNIA

*L*ocated in the heart of Sonoma County, the Inn at Occidental was once the oldest residential home in town. It was built in 1877 and converted to a B&B over 100 years later. This historic inn features a taste of yesteryear with its fir floors, wainscoted hallways, and spacious covered porches.

But access was not overlooked when the property was renovated. Says former owner Bill Bullard, "When the home was converted to an inn in 1988, a ground floor room was created to be accessible to anyone in a wheelchair."

The accessible Sugar Room takes its name from the collection of 19th-century sugar bowls that are displayed in the corner cabinet. The room features a level threshold, wide doorways, and good pathway access. It includes a gas fireplace, a king-sized bed and a spacious sitting area. The oversized bathroom has a roll-in shower with a hand-held showerhead and a built-in shower seat.

The Sugar Room features its own entrance from the English courtyard. The courtyard entrance is level and guests can access the rest of the ground floor from there. Accessible parking is located 40 feet from the courtyard entrance. There is a concrete walkway between the parking area and the Sugar Room.

The Sugar Room opens onto the ground floor where innkeepers Jerry and Tina Wolsbom host a nightly wine reception. Breakfast is served in the wine cellar, which is one floor down. Guests can choose to have breakfast in their room, the living room, their patio, or they can access the wine cellar from the outside via a ramped walkway.

Rates for the Sugar Room range from $195 to $229 per night.

The wine country is the major draw in the area, and many wineries have barrier-free access to their tasting rooms. The local winery map (www.wineroad.com) highlights those that are accessible. Sonoma is also known for its world-class restaurants, many of which are barrier-free.

Armstrong Redwoods State Reserve, located in nearby Guerneville, is also worth a visit. The reserve features a barrier-free interpretive trail that

The Sugar Room at the Inn at Occidental features a gas fireplace and a private courtyard entrance. (Photo courtesy of the Inn at Occidental.)

is less than 2/3 mile long and is easily accessible to power wheelchair-users. Some manual wheelchair-users may have a problem with the trail surface (which is a thick layer of duff), but there is also a paved road that winds throughout the park. It's a great way to get a close look at the magnificent redwoods.

Inn at Occidental
3657 Church Street
Occidental, CA 95465
(707) 874-1047
www.innatoccidental.com

Sleeping with the Animals

NORTHERN CALIFORNIA

*I*f you've ever dreamed of taking an African safari, check out these two unique Northern California safari-style B&Bs. Located about 170 miles from one another, Safari West and Vision Quest Ranch both offer visitors a real-life safari experience in luxury tents equipped with hardwood floors, electricity, and indoor plumbing. It's almost like visiting Africa; except you don't get jet lag, you save about $3,000, and you can do it in a weekend. And the good news is, both properties have accessible units.

Safari West is a 400-acre game preserve located just outside of Santa Rosa. It's home to a bevy of exotic animals and birds, many of which roam freely inside the gated compound. Safari West has two wheelchair-accessible safari tents, and two others that are suitable for slow walkers.

Tent 1H is the most accessible choice. It has a paved parking area, a ramped entry, wide doorways and ample room to maneuver a wheelchair. The bathroom features a roll-in shower with a fold-down shower seat, a hand-held showerhead, and grab bars in the shower and around the toilet.

Tent 2H is located up a slight dirt grade. It has the same access features as tent 1H except it has a grass parking area, and there are no toilet grab bars. Tents 3 and 4 are located near the dining area, have steps at the entry and are a good choice for slow walkers. All four of these tents have a roomy porch with great views of the giraffe enclosure. It's the ideal place to watch the sunset and enjoy a glass of wine.

And for a closer look at the Safari West residents, take the 2.5-hour safari tour. Half of the tour is a driving tour and the other half is a ranger-led walking tour. The standard tour is not wheelchair-accessible as you must climb up a few steps and transfer into a high safari vehicle. Wheelchair-users can request a modified tour, which covers the same area as the walking tour, but

Both of the accessible safari tents at Safari West have a spacious front porch.

includes transportation in a golf cart and a private guide. Advance reservations are required for all Safari West tours.

The nightly rate for the accessible tents at Safari West is $225. This rate includes a continental breakfast.

Vision Quest Ranch is located in the hills just outside of Salinas. This exotic-animal facility provides professionally trained animals to the film and television industry. Vision Quest Ranch is not a wildlife preserve. Their main business is animal training. The B&B, which is located next door, was set up to help support the animals.

The major difference between Safari West and Vision Quest Ranch is that Vision Quest Ranch is more remote. The tent cabins are far removed from the training facility, and there are no other buildings in the immediate vicinity. In fact, after you register at the gift shop, you have to drive back out to the main road and enter a separate gated area in order to reach the tent cabins.

The B&B consists of four safari-style tents that overlook the elephant playpen of the adjacent training facility. Giraffe Manor is the accessible tent, and as the name implies it is decorated in a giraffe motif. Accessible parking is available in a paved parking area a few hundred feet from the tent. Alternatively, you can park on the road in front of the tent.

Giraffe Manor at Vision Quest Ranch
features an accessible bathroom with a
roll–in shower.

There is ramp access to this spacious tent. Access features include wide doorways, a level threshold, and good pathway access throughout the tent. The bathroom has a roll-in shower with a fold-down shower seat, a hand-held showerhead, grab bars around the toilet and in the shower and a pedestal sink. There is also a refrigerator in the bathroom.

One of the highlights of staying at Vision Quest Ranch is breakfast, as it is usually delivered by elephant.

Giraffe Manor rents for $225 per night, and that rate includes breakfast.

One-hour walking tours of the animal training facility are also available for an additional charge. The tour is wheelchair-accessible, but manual wheelchair-users may require some assistance with one slight incline.

Safari West
3115 Porter Creek Road
Santa Rosa, CA 95404
(707) 579-2551
www.safariwest.com

Vision Quest Ranch
400 River Road
Salinas, CA 93908
(831) 455-1901
www.wildthingsinc.com

Breckenridge Picks

BRECKENRIDGE, COLORADO

Although Breckenridge is well known as a ski resort town, many visitors don't realize this mountain haven also offers a wide variety of year-round recreational opportunities. From skiing to mountain biking, there's something for everybody. And the good news is, many of these activities are accessible. Of course you also need an accessible place to rest your head, and in that respect two Breckenridge properties stand head-and-shoulders above the rest: the Allaire Timbers Inn and the Hunt Placer Inn.

Built from the ground up to be accessible, the Allaire Timbers Inn features 10 guest rooms, including the accessible Fremont Pass Lodge Room. Says innkeeper Kathy Gumph, "We did a lot of access research and had help

The accessible Freemont Pass Lodge Room at
Allaire Timbers Inn. (Photo by Todd Powell.)

*The Hunt Placer Inn features plenty of parking close
to the inn and level access to the front entrance.*

from a local architect when we were designing the inn. Plus we are continually learning from our disabled guests."

The Fremont Pass Lodge Room features wide doorways, touch lamps, and wheelchair-height furniture. Access features in the bathroom include a roll-in shower with a hand-held showerhead, grab bars in the shower area and around the toilet, a roll-under sink and a portable shower chair.

The inn also gets high marks for attitude. "One of our most important access features is our willingness to learn from each guest," says Kathy. "Over the years we have lengthened the door and window blind cords, moved the TV remote control to the nightstand, added kick plates to the room entry door and added an additional egg-crate mattress pad to the bedding. This was all done in response to guest feedback."

The Allaire Timbers Inn also has barrier-free access to the first-floor common rooms and level access to the scenic back deck. Accessible parking is located near the ramped entrance.

Nightly rates for the Fremont Pass Lodge Room range from $145 to $265. The highest rates are during Christmas week, and the lowest rates are from May to November.

The Hunt Placer Inn, another accessible choice, is tucked in the mountainside at the base of the Breckenridge Ski Resort. Trip and Kelly Butler, the second owners of the inn, purchased the property in 1999.

The previous owners installed an elevator and added the accessible Empress Room to the inn. And although the elevator was originally installed to accommodate guests who were injured on the slopes, it also provides excellent access for wheelchair-users and slow walkers.

The inn features level access to the front door and ample parking in the adjacent parking lot. The living room, dining room, and Empress Room are located on the second floor.

The Empress Room features Victorian decor and has wide doorways, a level threshold, lever handles and good pathway access. The bathroom has a tub/shower combination with a hand-held shower, grab bars in the shower and around the toilet, and a shower bench.

There is a hot tub on the redwood deck in the rear of the inn, and although there is level access to the deck, the hot tub itself does not have any access modifications.

Nightly room rates for the Empress Room range from $135 to $164.

Both innkeepers recommend Breckenridge Outdoor Education Center for accessible recreation opportunities. A top-rated adaptive ski program and a wheelchair-accessible ropes course are just a few of their offerings. Kelly adds, "The Breckenridge Ski Resort also hosts world-class adaptive ski programs throughout the winter."

Allaire Timbers Inn
9511 Highway 9 / South Main
Breckenridge, CO 80424
(970) 453-7530
www.allairetimbers.com

Hunt Placer Inn
275 Ski Hill Road
Breckenridge, CO 80424
(970) 453-7573
www.huntplacerinn.com

Old Town Guest House

COLORADO SPRINGS, COLORADO

*A*s a physical therapist, Kaye Caster understands access issues. So it's no big surprise that when she and her husband built their B&B, they went the full nine yards in the access department. Says Kaye "I hired an ADA consultant to advise me about access modifications before we began construction. After the B&B was completed he also wrote a brochure about all the access details of the room, so people with disabilities can see exactly what they are buying."

Built in 1997, the Old Town Guest House is a modern inn located in the historic district of Colorado Springs. There is level access to the front entrance and elevator access to all floors. The accessible African Orchid Room is located on the third floor.

A queen-sized bed complete with mosquito netting dominates the spacious African Orchid Room. Access features include wide doorways, good pathway access, lever hardware, a lowered closet rod, low-pile carpet, and lowered environmental controls. The room also has a refrigerator, a gas fireplace, and a private balcony with a hot tub.

The bathroom features a roll-in shower with a hand-held showerhead, grab bars in the shower and around the toilet, and a roll-under sink. A portable shower chair is available upon request.

There is barrier-free access to all of the public areas including the dining room, library, and foyer. A detailed access brochure, which includes a floor plan and measurements, is also available.

The nightly rate for the African Orchid Room is $200. This rate includes wine and hors d'oeuvres in the afternoon and a full breakfast each morning.

Kaye has a number of accessible sightseeing suggestions. "There are many things to do here," she says. "This neighborhood is wheelchair-friendly with curb-cuts and wide sidewalks. There are a lot of barrier-free shops, galleries and restaurants in the area. We are also close to many natural wonders, so I always suggest a scenic drive through the countryside. It's really beautiful!"

And as far as access at the inn is concerned, Kaye says, "We would not have considered doing the inn any other way. We want to provide an atmosphere that any and all guests will feel comfortable in, regardless of physical ability. I am a physical therapist and my husband is a physician, so we feel very dedicated to our plan."

Old Town Guest House
115 South 26th Street
Colorado Springs, CO 80904
(719) 632-9194
www.OldTown-GuestHouse.com

Uncompahgre B&B

MONTROSE, COLORADO

*B*illed as an inn for all seasons and all reasons, the Uncompahgre B&B is located six miles south of Montrose and 18 miles north of Ridgway, in the quiet Colorado countryside. Built in 1914, the building that houses this B&B was once the home of the Uncompahgre School. The school closed in 1989, and in 1992 Barbara and Richard Helm purchased the property and began what can only be described as an extensive remodeling project. In August of 1993 the Helms welcomed their first guests to the Uncompahgre B&B.

Says Barbara, "Prior to becoming innkeepers, Rich and I ran an architectural woodworking shop for 20 years together, so we had some experience in designing professional offices that were accessible." She adds, "It was pretty easy to make the B&B accessible when we remodeled, especially since all of the guest rooms and public spaces are located on the main level."

There is ramp access to the south porch, and barrier-free access to all of the first-floor public rooms and the accessible French Provincial Room. The bathroom has a large low-step shower with a hand-held showerhead, grab bars in the shower and around the toilet and a roll-under sink. A portable shower chair is available upon request.

There is barrier-free access to the living–dining room, which is actually the former gymnasium-auditorium. Wooden floors throughout this area make it easy going for wheelers. Outside, it's fairly level but there is a lot of pea gravel in the area, so rolling around can be difficult.

Nightly rates for the French Provincial Room range from $55 from November 1 to May 14, to $75 from May 15 to October 31.

The big attraction in this area of Colorado is the scenery. Says Barbara, "You don't even have to get our of your car to enjoy the beauty here. I encourage guests to take a drive and check out some of the more scenic places including the Black Canyon of the Gunnison National Park, Ridgway State Park, Telluride, Ouray, the Blue Mesa Reservoir, and the Grand Mesa with its forests and lakes."

"Of course," Barbara adds, "if you'd prefer a more active vacation, you can have that too. We had a paraplegic hunter who stayed with us last year, and he and his brother went hunting in his ATV every day. They had a great time."

Uncompahgre B&B
21049 Uncompahgre Road
Montrose, CO 81401
(970) 240-4000
www.uncbb.com

Sundance Trail
Guest Ranch

RED FEATHER LAKES, COLORADO

*I*nnkeeper Dan Morin sums up his feelings about access in one simple sentence. "Ramps are cheap, friendships are invaluable," he says. "I've really enjoyed many of our disabled guests, and if our ranch wasn't accessible I would have missed out on meeting some great people."

Ten years ago Ellen and Dan Morin were nurses, but today they are mostly cowboy and cowgirl. In 1999 they opened up the Sundance Trail Guest Ranch. Located only 100 miles from Denver, the Sundance Trail operates as a dude ranch during the summer season and as a B&B the rest of the year. Says Dan, "We see a lot of kids in the summer, but during the fall, winter, and spring (the romantic seasons) the majority of our guests are couples."

And as you can imagine (from Dan's opening quote) access is a high priority to him. Says Dan, "Of course the most accessible entrance is the front door. Everyone should be able to come in the front door!" Indeed, the main lodge features ramp access to the front door and barrier-free access to all the public rooms. The property boasts two accessible suites, the Apache Suite and the Buffalo Suite.

Both accessible rooms have wide doorways and plenty of room to maneuver a wheelchair or scooter. The two-bedroom Buffalo Suite is located on the first floor of the main lodge, and it has a private ramped porch in the back. The Apache Suite has one bedroom (with a loft for kids) and ramped access to the private entrance from the adjacent parking area.

Both suites have bathrooms with large roll-in showers and hand-held showerheads, roll-under sinks and grab bars in the shower and toilet areas. The roll-in showers have a small lip, but they are still doable for many people.

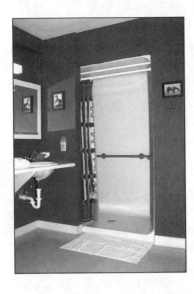

Although the large roll–in showers at Sundance Trail Guest Ranch have a small lip, they are still manageable for many people. (Photo courtesy of Sundance Trail Guest Ranch.)

Most of the outdoor public areas are accessible, with the exception of the chicken coop and the rabbit hutch. There are level dirt paths to the corrals and the arena. The recreation barn, which has a pool table, ping-pong table, VCR, and Jacuzzi, also has ramp access.

The nightly rates for the Buffalo Suite or the Apache Suite are $95 for double occupancy and $80 for single occupancy. These rates include a hearty country breakfast.

Dan is full of accessible sightseeing suggestions. "There's good trout fishing in Belaire Lake, which has ramp access and is only 15 minutes from here," he says.

Dan's other sightseeing suggestions include Fort Collins (45 minutes away) with lots of museums, small shops and restaurants, or Laramie (55 miles north) where you'll find the Wyoming Territorial Prison Museum and the U.S. Marshalls Museum.

But, admits Dan, "Most of our guests like to sit out on the deck and stargaze through the telescope. It's a favorite nighttime activity. You get a great look at the stars out here when you're away from all those city lights."

Sundance Trail Guest Ranch
17931 Red Feather Lakes Road
Red Feather Lakes, CO 80545
(970) 224-1222
www.SundanceTrail.com

Stonecroft Country Inn

LEDYARD, CONNECTICUT

Built in 1807, the Stonecroft Country Inn once enjoyed life as a sea captain's country estate. Today this 10-room inn, which is listed on the National Historic Register, includes a Georgian colonial main house and a recently renovated barn (the Grange). The main house features four large guest rooms, including the accessible Buttery, while the Grange houses six guest rooms and the dining room.

The Buttery has level access from both the inside and the outside. There is a brick walkway through the garden up to the Buttery's semiprivate deck, and level access to the room from there. Accessible parking is located at the foot of the walkway and a small hedge screens the deck. The front door of the Buttery opens to the Keeping Room of the main house, so guests can enjoy the large fireplace and have access to the three other public rooms.

The Buttery has wide doorways and good pathway access. In fact, it's been road tested by more than one wheeler, including the innkeeper's son. The room has a beamed ceiling and there are four wrought-iron hooks in the beams above the queen-sized bed. The hooks are functional as well as decorative. Says innkeeper Joan Egy, "My son uses the hooks to install his Hauser ropes." She adds, "He stays in the Buttery when he visits and it affords him great independence."

The bathroom has a tub/shower combination with a fold-down redwood bench and a hand-held shower. Although there's not a five-foot turning radius in the bathroom, it's still doable for many wheelers. You wheel in straight to use the sink, and transfer right to the tub or left to the toilet, and then back up to wheel out.

Breakfast is served in the Grange, which has level access. There is currently a gravel pathway over to the Grange, but Joan hopes to soon upgrade the surface to brick pavers.

Says Joan, "The disabled guests that have stayed with us so far were thrilled to be able to enjoy the ambiance of a historic inn, and we are happy we were able to accommodate them."

The nightly rate for the Buttery is $140.

The Stonecroft Country Inn is located just eight miles from Mystic Seaport. This 17-acre open-air museum features a large collection of historic ships and buildings. Although gravel roads and stone sidewalks are the norm throughout the waterfront area, many of the buildings are wheelchair-accessible. The Visitors' Center has an excellent access guide that describes the access to all of the buildings and attractions. Additionally, a limited number of manual wheelchairs are available for loan at the entrance.

Stonecroft Country Inn
515 Pumpkin Hill Road
Ledyard, CT 06339
(860) 572-0771
www.stonecroft.com

The Inn at Canal Square

LEWES, DELAWARE

*T*he Inn at Canal Square is located in the heart of historic downtown Lewes. This 24-room inn features great harbor views and generously sized guest rooms. And the good news is, access was incorporated into the inn when it was built, because the owners realized the need.

The side entrance is level and the doorway is wide enough to accommodate a wheelchair. The accessible entrance is approximately 15 feet from the accessible parking space. Room 205 is the accessible guest room.

There is elevator access to all floors, and Room 205 has wide doorways and good pathway access. The bathroom features a tub/shower combination with a hand-held shower and grab bars in the shower area and around the raised toilet.

The public areas of the inn feature barrier-free access. A complimentary continental breakfast is served in the ground-floor breakfast lounge, which is accessible via two French doors. The breakfast lounge has wheelchair-height tables, and the staff will gladly move any furniture that presents an access obstacle.

Nightly rates for Room 205 range from $115 to $245. The highest rates are during summer weekends, while the lowest rates are available on weekdays in January and February.

Top accessible sightseeing suggestions for the Lewes area include the Rehoboth Beach Factory Outlets and Cape Henlopen State Park.

Although wheeling around the historic district is difficult due to uneven pavement and intermittent curb-cuts, the Lewes Historic Society is worth a look if you can manage it. This interesting museum features a collection of old buildings which were relocated to this site. Most of the buildings have at least one step up, but you can see inside many of them from the accessible pathways throughout the complex.

If you'd like to shop till you drop, catch the lift-equipped trolley out to the Rehoboth Beach Factory Outlets. This whole shopping center features good access, and it's actually a better choice than historic Lewes for wheelchair-users.

And if you'd like to enjoy the great outdoors, head out to Cape Henlopen State Park. Here you'll find a three-mile paved trail, the accessible Seaside Nature Center, ramp access to the beach, level access to the fishing pier, and free loaner beach wheelchairs. It's a great (and very accessible) place to spend the day.

The Inn at Canal Square
122 Market Street
Lewes, DE 19958
(302) 644-3377
www.theinnatcanalsquare.com

Crane's Beach House

DELRAY BEACH, FLORIDA

*F*rom the beginning, Cheryl and Michael Crane realized access should not be an "optional" feature at their inn. In fact, they wanted to make sure everyone could enjoy all of the amenities at Crane's Beach House, so they paid close attention to access issues during the initial design of their property. When they finally welcomed their first guests to their 27-room luxury inn, this planning paid off.

Today, everybody can enjoy the blissful luxury of this unique property, which is nestled between the Atlantic Ocean and the Intracoastal Waterway in historic Delray Beach.

Crane's Beach House features a ramped front entrance, which is conveniently located next to the accessible parking area. The accessible guest room is called Bermuda.

Bermuda features wide doorways and good pathway access with lots of room to wheel around. This bungalow suite is decorated with murals of lush vegetation and features a separate living room, a small kitchen, and a secluded patio. The bathroom has a tub/shower combination with a built-in shower bench and grab bars.

All of the outdoor areas at Crane's Beach House are accessible, including the tiki huts, patio, outdoor grilling stations, and dining areas. The theme here is "enjoy the outdoors and live like the locals." It's a great place to just kick back and enjoy the warm weather.

The nightly rates for Bermuda range from $185 to $305. The lowest rates are available from May to October.

Favorite local activities include shopping and dining along "the Avenue" (Atlantic Avenue) in downtown Delray Beach. It's a nice place to wheel or stroll, and it's filled with sidewalk cafes, boutiques, and galleries.

Alternatively you can hit the beach at Delray Municipal Beach, which is just a half block from Crane's Beach House. Here you'll find accessible parking and ramp access to an elevated shelter and observation platform. And If you want to enjoy the sand and water, just borrow the beach wheelchair at the lifeguard station next to the shelter. It's a fun way to enjoy the day in Delray Beach.

Crane's Beach House
82 Gleason Street
Delray Beach, FL 33483
(561) 278-1700
www.cranesbeachhouse.com

Centennial House B&B

ST. AUGUSTINE, FLORIDA

*A*ccording to innkeeper Ellen Fugere, Centennial House combines the luxuries of the 21st century with the ambiance of the 19th century. After falling into disrepair many years ago, this 100-year-old gem underwent an extensive renovation by the previous owner. The renovation, which was competed in 1998, also included many access upgrades.

"We bought the inn and began operating it on August 23, 2002," says Ellen. "Having an accessible room was an important requirement in our search for a B&B, as this type of room is appealing to many guests."

This historic property features eight guest rooms, including the accessible Fleur de Lis Room. An accessible side entrance was also added during the renovation, and it provides ramp access from the parking area on the south side of the house. Says Ellen, "This is actually our main entrance as it's used by all of our staff and guests."

The first-floor Fleur de Lis Room features a queen-sized bed. Access features include wide doorways, good pathway access, lowered environmental controls, and a lowered closet rod. The bathroom has a roll-in shower with a hand-held showerhead, a pedestal sink and grab bars in the shower and around the toilet.

The first-floor public areas, including the dining room and the great room, also feature barrier-free access. The dining room is located right next to the Fleur de Lis Room, so it is very convenient for wheelchair-users and slow walkers. There is also a small courtyard near the end of the ramp in the back of the house. It's level and covered with brick pavers.

The nightly rates for the Fleur de Lis Room range from $120 to $165. The lowest rates are available Sunday through Thursday.

Centennial House is just two short blocks from St. George Street, which is the main street in the historic district. According to Ellen, most visitors enjoy exploring the shops and old homes in the historic district. It is a very pleasant area to walk or wheel around. As for accessible sightseeing suggestions, "The Fort is also nearby and it is accessible," says Ellen. "So are most of the museums.

"Centennial House is more than just a B&B," she adds. "We provide a welcoming, quiet and relaxing atmosphere with all the comforts of home. And I'm glad the previous owner was able to make this comfortable home accessible to everyone."

Centennial House B&B
26 Cordova Street
St. Augustine, FL 32084
(904) 810-2218
www.centennialhouse.com

Inn at the Bay

ST. PETERSBURG, FLORIDA

Although the Inn at the Bay was built in 1910, it wasn't always the charming property it is today. In fact, when innkeepers Dennis and Jewly Youschak first saw it, it was a residential hotel; and as Julie so delicately puts it, "Some of the residents weren't exactly pillars of the community."

After seven years of extensive remodeling, today this 12-room inn is decorated in Florida themes and features a number of access upgrades. Although there are steps at the front entrance, there is a new accessible entrance located in the rear, right next to the accessible parking space. This entrance was added during the renovation to provide convenient access to the inn.

The accessible Manatee Room is located on the first floor and includes a roll-in shower and a separate whirlpool tub. The double whirlpool tub is not wheelchair-accessible but it's a good option for an able-bodied companion. The bathroom also features grab bars in the shower and around the toilet, a hand-held showerhead, a roll-under sink and a five-foot turning radius. A shower chair is available upon request.

The centerpiece of the Manatee Room is the massive king-sized canopy bed, which is 25 inches high. Access features in the Manatee Room also include wide doorways, lever doorknobs, lowered light switches, and good pathway access. Dennis and Jewly will gladly move or remove any furniture upon request.

There is barrier-free access to all of the first-floor public areas, including the dining room, the lobby, and the living room.

The nightly rate for the Manatee Room is $165.

The Inn at the Bay makes an ideal base for exploring St. Petersburg, as it's within walking distance of many tourist attractions. Jewly is never at a loss for sightseeing suggestions. When I queried her about accessible and affordable sightseeing options, she immediately replied, "Take the Looper Trolley." I have to admit, it was an excellent suggestion.

The Manatee Room at the Inn at the Bay
features a massive, king-sized canopy bed.

The lift-equipped Looper Trolley runs a circular route in downtown St. Petersburg, and for 50 cents you can ride the entire route and get a good overview of the area. It also stops at some of St. Petersburg's major museums, including the St. Petersburg Museum of History, the Museum of Fine Arts, the Florida International Museum, the Florida Holocaust Museum, and the Salvador Dali Museum. These museums all feature a level entry and plenty of maneuvering space, so museum-hopping is another accessible sightseeing possibility.

Inn at the Bay
126 4th Avenue NE
St. Petersburg, FL 33701
(727) 822-1700
www.innatthebay.com

The Chanticleer Inn

LOOKOUT MOUNTAIN, GEORGIA

This 17-room inn sits atop Lookout Mountain near the Tennessee border and dates back to the 1930s. In 2002 Kirby and Judy Wahl entered the picture and lovingly restored the property to its former beauty. Says Judy, "It was previously in a state of decline, but it had a lot of charm. We really wanted to improve our community with this project."

Being astute business people, the Wahls also recognized the need for accessible lodging in the area. "We have a wedding facility across the street that is fully accessible and we wanted to be able to accommodate disabled guests here as well," says Judy. So the Wahls made sure to incorporate some access upgrades into their renovation project.

There are two level entrances to the main inn building, which houses the office, a common area, and two breakfast rooms. There are three steps between the front door and the common area, so it is not wheelchair-accessible. The accessible guest room (Room 14) is located in one of five detached stone cottages.

Room 14 is one of the larger rooms and it features a remodeled bathroom, two queen-sized beds, and an electric fireplace. There is ramp access to the room, and the bathroom features a roll-in shower with a hand-held showerhead. Guests have their choice of a continental breakfast at the inn (which has several steps) or a full breakfast at the nearby Big Rock Cafe (which has ramped access).

The 1.5 acres that surround the inn are filled with paved trails and stone paths, many of which are suitable for wheelchairs. There is also ramp access to the outdoor pool area.

The nightly rate for Room 14 ranges from $140 to $155.

Rock City is one of the biggest attractions in the area, and it's located right across the street from the inn. The accessible tour takes visitors on a half-mile round-trip walk to the overlook at Lover's Leap and the Flag Court.

Since only a portion of the garden is accessible, there is a reduced price for the tour.

Judy also recommends the Tennessee Aquarium, the IMAX Theater and the Incline Railway, all of which have at least partial wheelchair access. Says Judy, "There's lots to do in the area, and we do our best to host all of our guests."

The Chanticleer Inn
1300 Mockingbird Lane
Lookout Mountain, GA 30750
(706) 820-2002
www.stayatchanticleer.com

The Guest House at Volcano

VOLCANO, HAWAII

Billed as a "private village nestled on six acres of the native high-altitude rain forest," The Guest House at Volcano first opened for business in 1985. This unique lodging option currently has three wheelchair-accessible units, but innkeepers Bonnie Goodell and Alan Miller agree that more access upgrades are always a future possibility.

"Claudia's Place is an accessible apartment we built for my mother-in-law (Claudia) who had a Parkinson's-like disability. It convinced me that everything should be accessible, if possible," says Bonnie.

Twin I and Twin II at the Guest House at Volcano
feature a spacious living area with two twin beds.

Built in 1995, Claudia's Place features ramped access from the paved driveway. There are no designated parking spaces, but there is plenty of room to park a van near the base of the ramp. The parking area is only 10 feet from Claudia's Place.

Claudia's Place shares a front porch with the main house and features a queen-sized bed in the bedroom and a twin bed in the living area. There is also a small kitchen in the unit. Access features include wide doorways, wooden floors, and good pathway access. The bathroom has a low-step shower with a hand-held showerhead and grab bars in the shower. There are adjustable grab bars (which can be lifted up out of the way for transfers) on both sides of the toilet. A portable shower bench is available upon request.

Bonnie and Alan also kept access in mind when they added their next units in 2001. Twin I and Twin II mirror one another and share a large covered porch. Each unit has a bedroom alcove with a queen-sized bed, a spacious living room with two twin beds, a kitchen area, and a large bathroom. The Twins each have a low-step shower, a hand-held showerhead, grab bars in the shower and around the toilet, and a portable shower bench. Parking is available directly in front of the Twins, but some people will need assistance navigating through the gravel.

Bonnie may also be able to provide special equipment (such as a hospital bed or a manual wheelchair) with advance notice. "We have a community lending closet here, which sometimes has medical equipment," says Bonnie. "Last week I was able to borrow a manual wheelchair for a guest. It all depends on what is available, but it never hurts to ask."

There is no formal breakfast served at The Guest House at Volcano, but breakfast fixings are available on the front porch 24 hours a day. The front porch has ramp access, and guests can enjoy a cup of coffee there or take breakfast makings back to their own unit.

The nightly rate for Claudia's Place is $85. The Twins rent for $95 (each) per night. These rates are for two people. For each additional adult add $15, and for each additional child (under 13) add $10.

The Guest House at Volcano has an excellent location, just five minutes from Hawaii Volcanoes National Park. Accessible sights within the park include the Kilauea Visitor Center, the Volcano House Hotel and Restaurant, the Jaggar Museum, and the Volcano Art Center. It's possible to drive along Kilauea's caldera on Crater Rim Drive, and then look down into the crater at the Jaggar Museum overlook. The Chain of Craters Road also makes a very scenic drive, but most of the overlooks are not accessible. And don't miss the Earthquake Trail, just left of the Volcano House Hotel. This half-mile asphalt trail is what's left of the road that once circled the Caldera. It was closed to vehicle traffic after a 1983 eruption and earthquake, but today it offers pedestrians a prime view of the crater.

The Guest House at Volcano
P.O. Box 6
Volcano, HI 96785
(808) 967-7775
www.volcanoguesthouse.com

Blue Heron Inn

I first met Claudia Klinger at a conference in Chicago. Claudia was interested in learning more about marketing the accessible features of her Blue Heron Inn, and as luck would have it, I was giving a seminar on that very subject. Claudia proved an excellent student as she asked intelligent questions and took copious notes. Several months later I visited her website and was thrilled to discover she had added detailed access information about her property. After all, if you expect to book your accessible rooms, you can't very well keep your access a secret!

Claudia impressed me right from the start with her progressive attitude about access. "My husband and I previously worked in corporate management, and we often saw disabled employees struggle with inaccessible workplace facilities," she said. "So, when we built our inn, wheelchair accessibility was one of our design considerations. We wanted everybody to be able to enjoy the amenities of our property."

The Blue Heron Inn was completed in 2000, and it was named after the birds that frequent the nearby Snake River. This western-designed inn is situated on over three acres, and features 640 feet of prime river frontage. The inn has six guest rooms, including the very accessible Bunk House Room.

There is ramp access to the inn, and accessible parking is available at the foot of the ramp. The first-floor Bunk House Room is decorated with cowboy boots, hats, and handcrafted pine furniture. It has a queen-sized bed, wide doorways and good pathway access. The bathroom features a roll-in shower with a hand-held showerhead and grab bars in the shower and around the toilet. This room also has a great view of the trestle bridge over the river.

All of the first-floor public rooms and porches feature barrier-free access. There are two other first-floor guest rooms, but neither has any access adaptations. These rooms may be suitable for people who cannot climb a whole flight of stairs. The grounds around the inn are fairly level and there is an accessible trail along the top of the levee.

The nightly rates for the Bunk House Room range from $99 to $119.

The Blue Heron Inn is just a 90-minute drive from Yellowstone and Grand Teton National Parks. One of the big attractions in the area (and around the inn) is the abundance of wildlife, including white-tail deer, an occasional moose, beavers, wild turkeys, bald eagles, herons, ospreys, and owls.

Says Claudia, "We spent 10 years dreaming about and planning the inn and we are very pleased that we fulfilled our dream. The inn has many objects that we made ourselves, such as handmade quilts, woodwork, lamps, and needlework. Everyone who stays here seems to love it."

Blue Heron Inn
4175 East Menan Lorenzo Highway
Rigby, ID 83442
(208) 745-9922
www.idahoblueheron.com

Cloran Mansion

When you mention B&Bs in the Midwest, the conversation inevitably turns to Galena, Illinois. Besides boasting a large collection of period mansions that have been converted to B&Bs, Galena also has a thriving population of artists and craftspeople as well as a relaxed small-town atmosphere. In short, it just oozes charm. Add location to that delicate mix—it's just a three-hour drive from nearby Chicago—and you can begin to understand why Galena gets top marks from the B&B crowd.

Former Chicago resident Cheryl Farruggia also gives Galena top marks. "I dreamed about owning a B&B in Galena for about 20 years," she recalls. "The plan was to begin my search when I turned 50, but I didn't quite make it. One weekend I was visiting friends in Galena and I decided to go look at B&Bs with a realtor. I had no intention of buying, but when I saw the Cloran Mansion I fell in love. On August 6, 2001, my husband and I became innkeepers."

Today Cheryl and Carmine welcome visitors to their 1880 Italianate Victorian mansion, located just across the street from the Galena water tower. Cloran Mansion has five guest rooms; four in the main house plus a detached cottage. Although there is one step up to the main house, the cottage was constructed to be barrier-free. "I was in health care for 25 years, so the fact that the cottage is accessible is very important to me," says Cheryl.

Built in 1996, Antonio's Cottage measures a very spacious 570-square feet and has heated floors, a three-sided fireplace, and a double whirlpool. There are no designated parking places at the mansion, but there's plenty of room to park right outside of the cottage. A level pathway leads to the front door of the cottage.

Access features in the cottage include wide doorways, a level threshold, good pathway access, and hardwood floors. The bathroom has a roll-in shower with a hand-held showerhead and a built-in shower seat. Other features include a roll-under sink and grab bars around the toilet and in the shower.

The cottage also has a kitchen area with a table and three chairs, a refrigerator, a coffee pot, a microwave and dishes. A full country-style breakfast is

Antonio's Cottage at the Cloran Mansion features level access through wide French doors at the front entrance.

served each morning in the main house, but it can be delivered to the cottage upon request.

The grounds around Cloran Mansion are quite pleasant. A sidewalk leads from the parking area to the new screened-in gazebo. The sidewalk is uneven in a few places, but it's still doable for most people. The 14-foot octagon gazebo features a wide doorway with a level threshold. It's a great place to enjoy a glass of wine and relax in the evening.

Says Cheryl, "We have had at least four honeymooners who needed an accessible room stay in Antonio's Cottage. If we hadn't had the cottage, they would not have been able to experience our B&B."

Rates for Antonio's Cottage range from $189 to $225 per night.

The big attraction in Galena is Main Street, which is packed full of galleries, shops, and restaurants. The downtown area has wide sidewalks and curb-cuts at every corner. Some of the shops have one step at the entry, but many others are accessible. To be honest, it's quite pleasant to just stroll along Main Street, window-shop, and take in the ambiance of the historic town.

Cloran Mansion
1237 Franklin Street
Galena, IL 61036
(815) 777-0583
www.cloranmansion.com

Hawk Valley Retreat

GALENA, ILLINOIS

*A*lthough Hawk Valley Retreat calls Galena home, this country proper-ty is actually located well outside of the city proper. And in my book, that's a very good thing. That's why it's called a retreat, as it's a place where you can just sit back and relax, enjoy nature, and leave the hustle and bustle of the rest of the world behind.

Innkeepers Jane and Fritz Fuchs both understand this need for peace and quiet, as that's what first attracted them to country life. They also under-stand how important a quiet atmosphere is to their guests. In fact, Jane won't even mow the lawn when she has guests. "You hear those lawnmower noises all the time in the city," she quipped. "You don't need to hear them when you come out here!"

Don't get me wrong: even though it's secluded, you don't exactly have to rough it at Hawk Valley Retreat. The property offers some very luxurious amenities, and as a bonus it's situated on 10 secluded acres with a pond, walking trail, and gardens. It's a bird-watchers paradise, and yes, they really do have hawks.

Hawk Valley Retreat offers several accessible options, including a B&B room in the main house and several private cottages.

The Swan Lake Room is located in the main house. It has a private entrance from the wraparound deck, or you can enter through the house. There is ramp access to the office and house and plenty of room to maneuver a wheelchair inside. The Swan Lake bathroom features a roll-in shower, grab bars, a roll-under sink and a five-foot turning radius. A shower chair is avail-able upon request.

If you'd like a little more privacy and a lot more room, check out one of the newly constructed cottages. Fritz built the cottages from the ground up, and he continues to make improvements to the property today. Jane jokes, "I don't just have a honey-do list, I have a honey-do binder!" Joking aside, Fritz is very proud of his work, and happy he was able to include some access features in the cottages.

Fox Glen Cottage is the most accessible choice as it has an adapted bathroom, and it's the cottage that's closest to the main house. Accessible parking is available directly in front of the cottage, and access features include wide doorways, level thresholds, and an open floor plan with excellent pathway access.

The bathroom features a roll-in shower with a fold-down shower seat and a hand-held showerhead. Other access features include grab bars, a pedestal sink and a full five-foot turning radius.

Fox Glen has a long list of amenities including a king-sized bed, a two-person Jacuzzi tub, a fold-out sleeper sofa, a kitchenette, a private porch, and a fireplace. Just pick up a few groceries and you'll never have to leave the retreat.

The Pines Cottage offers the same access features as Fox Glen, except this cottage is located a little farther from the main house. Somerset, Fritz's newest masterpiece, is located even farther from the main house (up a slight incline) and it has a double whirlpool tub in place of the roll-in shower. This cottage is not adapted for access, but it may work for some slow walkers, as it's just as roomy as the other two cottages.

The most accessible cottage at Hawk Valley Retreat is Fox Glen Cottage,
which features a king–sized bed, a gas fireplace, and a spacious living area.

Although the whole property is not accessible, there are many level areas to explore. A golf cart is also available for slow walkers.

Nightly rates for the Swan Lake Room range from $85 to $98. Rates for the Fox Glen, Pines, and Somerset cottages range from $160 to $185 per night. All rates include breakfast.

Hawk Valley Retreat is also the home of the Hawk Valley School of the Arts, which offers one- to five-day workshops taught by local artists. Subjects include basketweaving, painting, watercolors, and quilting, and they are offered in a range of skill levels. Visit the retreat website for current offerings or give Jane a call for a catalogue. It's a great way to get away from the city and spend a few days, so as Jane says, "Come, stay, enjoy and relax."

Hawk Valley Retreat
2752 West Cording Road
Galena, IL 61036
(815) 777-4100
www.hawkvalleyretreat.com

Columbus Inn

COLUMBUS, INDIANA

*I*f you're interested in historic Midwestern architecture, then the Columbus Inn is just the property for you. Built in 1895, the building was designed by architect Charles F. Sparrell to serve as the town's first City Hall. Today the property is listed on the Registry of Historic Landmarks and noted as one the few remaining examples of Victorian Romanesque architecture in the city.

After sitting vacant for several years, the building was restored and converted to a B&B in 1986. Many of the original features were preserved during the restoration, including ceramic tiles in the lobby, tin ceilings on the first and third floors, and most of the original moldings and trim. Although this 34-room inn is filled with Victorian antiques and exudes an ambiance of yesteryear, modern access features were also added during the renovation.

Says General Manager Chester Dingus, "When the building was converted into a B&B it was decided to incorporate wheelchair access as well, so as to best appeal to a wide range of visitors."

The most accessible entrance is located on the side. There are eight steps leading to the door, but a ramp was added to accommodate wheelchairs and walkers. This is also the most convenient entrance as it's located adjacent to the inn's parking lot. Inside there is elevator access to all floors.

The inn has two accessible guestrooms, which feature wide doorways, good pathway access, and lowered closet rods. Each room has two full-size beds and a desk work area. The bathrooms each have a tub/shower combination with grab bars, a portable shower chair, and grab bars around the toilet.

All public areas, including the breakfast room, also feature barrier-free access.

Nightly room rates range from $109 to $289.

"The biggest attraction in Columbus is the historic architecture throughout the city," says Chester. The Columbus Area Visitors Center conducts guided walking tours that include many of the city's historic structures. "Another good option for wheelchair-users is a self-guided walking tour," adds Chester. "We have maps available at the inn. Visitors can still enjoy the architecture, but they can do it at their own pace on the self-guided tour."

Columbus Inn
445 Fifth Street
Columbus, In 47201
(812) 378-4289
www.thecolumbusinn.com

Amish Country Inns

ELKHART COUNTY, INDIANA

*P*art of the charm of Northern Indiana Amish country lies in the simple lifestyle of the Amish people. And although visitors can't exactly spend the night with an Amish family, they can enjoy a taste of their country lifestyle at many inns and B&Bs throughout Elkhart County. Here are a few accessible choices.

First stop, the Essenhaus Country Inn in Middlebury. This 40-room inn is part of Essenhaus Village; an Amish-themed village that includes everything from a restaurant and a bakery to an animal farm and a covered bridge. The whole complex is nicely done with paved paths, curb-cuts, and level access to the buildings.

The Essenhaus Country Inn features spacious rooms with plenty of country charm.

The two-story inn is located near the middle of the complex and features accessible parking and barrier-free access to the ground floor. Room 112 is accessible. It is located on the ground floor and has wide doorways, lever handles, and good pathway access. The bathroom features a tub/shower combination with grab bars in the shower and around the toilet. A shower chair is available upon request.

The public areas of the inn are barrier-free and very inviting. In fact, the homey lobby and front porch are great places to relax after dinner and enjoy a cookie from the community cookie jar.

The rate for Room 112 is $99 per night.

Down the road in Millersburg, The Big House in the Little Woods is surrounded by Amish farms and located in a very scenic part of the county. It gets high marks for access, as innkeeper Sarah Stoltzfus has first-hand experience with access issues. In fact, their accessible room (The Suite) was originally designed for Sarah's mom.

Says Stoltzfus, "We made a small apartment wheelchair-friendly for my mother. After she passed away, we redecorated it and added it to our B&B inventory." The Suite includes a ramped entry, wide doorways, and barrier-free pathway access. There is a separate sitting area with a recliner and a sofa bed, and the bedroom can be configured with either a king-sized bed or two twins. The bathroom has a roll-in shower with a hand-held showerhead, a roll-under sink, grab bars by the toilet and in the shower, and a plastic shower bench.

Rates for The Suite range from $70 to $90 per night.

Elkhart County makes a great road-trip destination. Be sure and stop at the Amish Country Visitors Center in Elkhart and pick up the Heritage Trail Tour audio tape. This 90-minute tape is filled with interesting stories about the history of the area and the Amish people, and it contains driving directions and information about local landmarks and tourist sights. There's no charge for the tape, but visitors are asked to leave a $20 refundable deposit.

And if you're in the area on the fourth Saturday of September, don't miss the annual Quilt Auction at the Mennonite Relief Sale. Local crafters donate handmade quilts which are auctioned off to the highest bidders. This popular event is held at the Elkhart County Fairgrounds in Goshen, which has accessible parking and restrooms, and level access to the fair's buildings.

Essenhaus Country Inn
240 U.S. Highway 20
Middlebury, IN 46540
(574) 825-9471
www.essenhaus.com

The Big House in the Little Woods
4245 South 1000 W
Millersburg, IN 46543
(260) 593-9076
www.bighouselittlewoods.com

Inntiquity

LOGANSPORT, INDIANA

*B*illed as a country inn and B&B housed in a renovated 1849 dairy barn, Inntiquity is located on 23 acres of Indiana meadow land, just 35 miles from Purdue. But don't let the dairy barn fool you! In reality, this property is quite luxurious and very accessible.

Says innkeeper Lee Naftzger, "When we created our inn, it just seemed natural to include ramps, accessible bathrooms, and wheelchair-access so we could welcome all travelers."

The inn features ramp access to the side door from the adjacent parking lot, and a front entrance with a wide double-doorway and a low sill. The Victorian Suite and the Wood Violet Suite are both located on the ground floor, and each offers a different level of access.

The Victorian Suite is the most accessible choice, and it features wide doorways and good pathway access. This two-room suite has one queen-sized bed and one standard bed. The large bathroom has a roll-in shower, a portable shower bench, and a roll-under sink.

The Wood Violet Suite is a good choice for slow walkers as it has ground floor access but no adapted bathroom. This two-room suite features a king-sized bed and a separate sitting room. The bathroom has a two-person corner Jacuzzi with a shower. There are grab bars around the Jacuzzi, but they are primarily for balance and safety, rather than for transfers.

The ground floor public areas all have barrier-free access. There is also an accessible public restroom on the ground floor.

The nightly rate for the Victorian Suite is $100. The Wood Violet Suite rents for $125 per night.

Lee is full of local sightseeing suggestions. "We are located at the confluence of the Eel and Wabash Rivers and we have many scenic drives around here," she says. "Riverside Park has a famous Dentzel carousel and

Logansport also has a performing arts program and a civic theater that attracts visitors. The Ironhorse festival in July celebrates our railroad history, and it's a very popular event."

Inntiquity
1075 State Road 25 North
Logansport, IN 46947
(574) 722-2398
www.inntiquity.com

Home Farm B&B

*H*ome Farm Resort offers a variety of country accommodations, including a B&B, cottages, campsites, and a farmhouse for family reunions. The five-room B&B is housed in a 1940s-era farm house and located on the family farm of Roswell and Elizabeth Garst.

Back in 1959, during the height of the Cold War, the Garsts welcomed Soviet premier Nikita Khrushchev to their rural Iowa farm. This historic event opened the doors to the "trade butter, not guns" diplomacy between the Soviet Union and the United States.

Today this working farm continues to welcome guests from all over the world. In 1997, after Elizabeth died at the ripe old age of 101, her granddaughter opened up the B&B. Says Innkeeper Liz Garst, "This house belonged to my grandmother, and I know she would have wanted the B&B to be wheelchair-accessible."

The accessible Harvest Room is located on the ground floor and has wide doorways, good pathway access, and a queen-sized bed. The bathroom has a roll-in shower with a hand-held showerhead and a fold-down shower seat. There are also grab bars in the shower and around the toilet.

All of the first-floor public rooms, including the dining room and the living room, have barrier-free access. The front entrance has a wide doorway and a level threshold. The yard and garden areas are relatively flat and easy to negotiate in a wheelchair.

The nightly rate for the Harvest Room is $90.

"Many of our disabled guests enjoy exploring the beautiful 4,500-acre property by John Deere gator [a utility vehicle]," says Liz." We also offer draft-horse wagon rides. There are three steps to the hayrack, and many slow walkers enjoy that experience. Our astronomy tour, which is offered two weekends a month, is wheelchair-accessible, as is my Khrushchev History Talk."

Accessible options in town include the municipal aquatic center, which has a zero-step beach, and the two-mile asphalt hiking trail at Riverside Park. Liz adds, "Madison County, with its famous covered bridges, lies just 70 miles southeast of Coon Rapids. It's a very scenic drive."

Home Farm B&B
1390 Highway 141
Coon Rapids, IA 50058
(712) 684-2964
www.farmresort.com

Mandolin Inn

DUBUQUE, IOWA

*B*uilt in 1908, the Mandolin Inn is a 27-room historic mansion that has been lovingly restored to its former grandeur. The inn takes its name from the unusual leaded-glass window on the first landing of the grand oak staircase. This rare Tiffany treasure depicts Saint Cecelia, patron saint of musicians, holding a mandolin.

The inn is filled with antiques and has eight guest rooms, including one that is wheelchair-accessible: another rare find in a period home. Says innkeeper Amy Boynton, "My mother was a quadriplegic, and I had always planned to make my inn accessible to wheelchairs once I bought it. I wanted to make a lovely accessible guest room with all the amenities that one would expect in this beautiful mansion and I'm happy to say that that is what the Pond's Edge room is."

Access renovations actually began on the outside as Amy added a bridge and a ramp that winds through a small garden, over the goldfish pond and right up to the accessible entrance. This attractive ramp not only provides access, it's also aesthetically pleasing.

The Pond's Edge guest room is on the first floor, near the goldfish pond. It features a queen-sized bed and a gas fireplace and has wide doorways, lever handles, and good pathway access. In fact, the whole room had to be enlarged once the 60"-wide roll-in shower was delivered. "It was huge," exclaimed Amy. "At that point I decided to knock out the kitchen pantry so there would be more room in the accessible bathroom."

The bathroom features a five-foot turning radius, a roll-under sink, grab bars by the toilet and in the shower, a hand-held showerhead and a fold-down shower seat. The roll-in shower has a level threshold (no lip), a detail that is often overlooked in a lot of renovations. The whole room is very nicely done, and Amy credits her success to doing a lot of research and to finding a contractor who was well educated about accessible design.

The first-floor public areas are equally accessible, with wide doorways, plenty of pathway access, and a small ramp out to the large wraparound

The 27-room Mandolin Inn has been lovingly restored
to its former grandeur by innkeeper Amy Boynton.

porch. The most unusual feature of the home? The oil painting wall paper in the dining room. Don't miss it.

The nightly rate for Pond's Edge is $130.

Amy is full of suggestions for accessible sightseeing in the area. Her top pick is the new America's River project at the Port of Dubuque. Here you'll find the Mississippi Riverwalk, the Diamond Jo Casino, the Spirit of Dubuque, and the Mississippi River Museum and Aquarium.

All of these attractions offer good access; however, my personal favorite is the Mississippi River Museum and Aquarium. This Smithsonian-affiliated museum features interpretive exhibits about the wildlife found in the river and tells the story of the early Mississippi River explorers. It's one of the best museums I've ever visited, and it's reason enough to plan a visit to Dubuque.

Mandolin Inn
199 Loras Boulevard
Dubuque, IA 52001
(563) 556-0069
www.mandolininn.com

Benham
Schoolhouse Inn

BENHAM, KENTUCKY

As its name implies, the Benham Schoolhouse Inn was previously a schoolhouse. Built in 1926, this national historic landmark was converted to an inn by the Southeast Education Foundation in an effort to preserve the mining heritage of the region and to attract tourism dollars to the community. Thankfully, much of the old school ambiance remains after the conversion, including the nostalgic hallway lockers.

During the conversion, access upgrades were added, but because of the historic status of the building, the original facade and entry (with steps) remains. There is accessible parking on the side of the building, but it's best to drive around to the back lot, as the accessible entrance is located there. From there you can access all of the first-floor public rooms, except the meeting room, which has a separate accessible entrance.

There are two accessible first-floor guestrooms (1937, 1939), and although they have different furnishings and decor, they are identical access-wise. Both rooms have level thresholds, wide doorways, and good pathway access. Each bathroom has a low-step shower with a built-in shower seat. A roll-under sink is located in the bedroom.

Although there is plenty of room for a wheelchair to maneuver in the bathroom, these rooms are best suited for a slow walker (or somebody who can walk a few steps to transfer) because of a few design features in the bathrooms. Because of the placement of the built-in shower benches (on the back wall) a direct transfer is difficult without a shower chair. Additionally, there is only one toilet grab bar and it is located in front of the toilet (on the side wall). Again this would make a direct transfer to the toilet very difficult. Still these are very nice rooms for anybody who can walk a few steps.

There is also barrier-free access to the Apple Room Restaurant, which is located across the hall from the office.

Rooms 1937 and 1939 each rent for $70 per night.

As for accessible sightseeing options, Bruce Ayers, President of Southeast Community College recommends the nearby Kentucky Coal Mining Museum. Benham was once the company town of Wisconsin Steel, and the Kentucky Coal Mining Museum occupies the former company store on Main Street.

The museum presents a comprehensive look at coal mining history and also features a few fun exhibits like a kids' coal mine (which is just the right height for wheelers) and a collection of Loretta Lynn memorabilia. Access is good throughout the museum, with a level entry, accessible restrooms, and elevator access to all floors.

Lynch, just two miles down the road, is also worth a visit; if only to look at the architecture in this former U.S. Steel company town. And be sure to check out Portal 31 while you're in town. Currently this coal mine tour is not very accessible, but future plans call for wheelchair-accessible transportation into the mine. Quite possibly it will be the first wheelchair-accessible coal mine in the world.

Benham Schoolhouse Inn
100 Central Avenue
Benham, KY 40807
(606) 848-3000
www.kingdomcome.org/inn

Room 1937 at the Benham Schoolhouse Inn is located on the ground floor and has plenty of room to maneuver a wheelchair.

The Historic French Market Inn

NEW ORLEANS, LOUISIANA

*B*uilt in the 1800s for Baron Joseph Xavier de Pontalba, The Historic French Market Inn features 95 rooms and suites, a lush courtyard, and one of the best locations in the French Quarter. Located on the corner of Decatur and St. Louis streets, this renovated property is within rolling distance of most of the major French Quarter attractions. And although there are some access obstacles in this historic section of town, Decatur is one of the most accessible streets.

Parking is at a premium in the French Quarter, but there's a large public parking lot with plenty of accessible spaces conveniently located right across the street from the inn. The Historic French Market Inn features wide doorways, a level entry, and elevator access to all floors. There is good pathway access to the private courtyard and plenty of room to wheel around the lobby and the other public areas.

The accessible guest room has wide doorways, a level threshold, and good pathway access. It has an open-framed double-sized bed, lowered closet rods, and lever hardware. The bathroom features a tub/shower combination with a hand-held showerhead, grab bars in the shower and around the toilet, a roll-under sink and a plastic shower bench.

All in all, they've done a very nice job with the access features in this historic property.

Rates at The Historic French Market Inn start at just $79 per night, and they vary greatly with the season. You'll find the highest rates and the lowest availability during the annual Mardi Gras celebration.

As you can imagine, there are plenty of diversions in the French Quarter. The good news is, many of them are accessible. The Historic French Market Inn is located just two blocks from Jackson Square, the Louisiana State Museum, and Café Du Monde, all of which offer good wheelchair access. Your best bet is to stop in at the New Orleans Convention and Visitors Bureau, just across from Jackson Square, and pick up your free French Quarter Self-Guided Walking Tour Map. You can do the tour at your own pace and choose an alternate route if you encounter any access obstacles.

If you'd prefer a guided tour, Gray Lines Tours offers a variety of city tours in lift-equipped vehicles. Alternatively, you can see New Orleans by boat aboard the steamboat Natchez. There is ramp access to the boat, but only stairway access between the decks. All in all it's a good cruise and a fun way to get a different glimpse of New Orleans.

The Historic French Market Inn
501 Rue Decatur
New Orleans, LA 70130
(504) 5561-5621
www.frenchmarketinn.com

Maine Seaside Inns

Because of its strategic North Atlantic location, Maine has a long and proud maritime history. With scenic roads and quaint towns scattered along the rugged coastline, it's a great place to learn about this history and enjoy the coastal beauty. And since we have a theme going here, you'll undoubtedly want to hole up in a quaint seaside inn during your visit. Although Maine boasts more than its fair share of inns, two south-coast properties stand out as far as access and ambiance are concerned.

Located in Boothbay Harbor, the Harbour Towne Inn is a good choice for slow walkers. This Victorian inn specializes in old-fashioned "Downeast" hospitality, and innkeeper George Thomas makes everybody feel welcome. "My grandfather was disabled," says George. "I remember his trials and tribulations when he traveled. He never complained, God bless him. I just wanted to make things a little easier for disabled folks who travel, so we did what we could to make our historic inn accessible."

The Harbour Towne Inn has two rooms suitable for slow walkers. Both rooms (Room 7 and Room 8) are located on the ground floor, and they feature low-step showers with a two-inch step. There are grab bars in the shower, and a portable shower chair is available upon request.

It's important to note that there are two steps at the front entrance to the inn. Says George, "The main door usually requires some assistance to enter, and we are working on this." Breakfast is usually served on the outside deck, and the staff is happy to assist guests and carry food outside or move any furniture that may be in the way. Breakfast can also be delivered to your room upon request.

The nightly rates for Room 7 and Room 8 range from $99 to $149 in the low season and from $169 to $199 in the high season.

The Inn at Bath, which is located just 22 miles down the road, is a good option for wheelchair-users. This 1810 Greek Revival home is located on a tree-lined street in the heart of Bath's historic district, and it's within easy walking distance of charming shops and excellent restaurants.

Former owner Nick Bayard added the accessible Garden Room in 1995. "I built the Garden Room with large lime-stained structural beams and wide pine floorboards," says Nick. This first-floor room features a private ramped entrance, which leads through the garden from the Washington Street entrance.

The Garden Room has wide doorways, good pathway access, a king-sized bed and a sofa daybed. The bathroom has a tub/shower combination with a hand-held shower, a roll-under sink, a raised toilet, and grab bars in the shower and on one side of (but not behind) the toilet. A wooden seat, which can be placed across the top of the tub, is also available.

Breakfast is served in the dining room, which is located right next door to the Garden Room.

Nightly room rates at The Inn at Bath range from $100 to $175 in the low season and from $150 to $185 in the high season.

As far as accessible area attractions go, both innkeepers agree the Maine Maritime Museum tops the list. Located on the grounds of the former Percy & Small Shipyard in Bath, this museum offers visitors a comprehensive look at the local shipbuilding and seafaring history. The museum not only houses a large collection of maritime artwork and artifacts, it also features interpretive exhibits in the restored shipyard buildings.

There is ramped access to the main museum building, and barrier-free access throughout the galleries. Outside, there are asphalt and dirt paths throughout the shipyard; however, there are a few inclines that may be difficult for manual wheelchair–users. A golf cart is available for loan to those who may have problems with the distance or the terrain. It's really a great museum, and truly one of Maine's "don't miss" attractions.

Harbour Towne Inn
71 Townsend Avenue
Boothbay Harbor, ME 04538
(207) 633-4300
www.harbourtowneinn.com

The Inn at Bath
969 Washington Street
Bath, ME 04530
(207) 443-4294
www.innatbath.com

Harraseeket Inn

*S*ome innkeepers put a very high priority on access. Take Chip Gray, of the Harraseeket Inn for example. Says Chip, "We have discovered that the ADA rules are actually only the tip of the iceberg." Indeed, not many historic inns have a pool with a lift, like the Harraseeket Inn. And to borrow a quote from Chip, that's really just the tip of the iceberg.

Located on Main Street in downtown Freeport, the Harraseeket Inn encompasses two period buildings that were built in 1795 and 1850, plus a new wing that was added in 1989. This 84-room inn features accessible parking near the back entrance, elevator access to all floors, and a barrier-free pathway through the perennial garden.

The Gray family first opened the Harraseeket Inn as a five-room B&B in 1982. Throughout the years they have made many additions and renovations, but they have always been very mindful of access issues. Chip's mother, Nancy Gray, remembers the early days. "Access issues were very confusing back then," she recalls. "Sometimes the federal and the state access regulations were different. I ended up doing a lot of research on the subject and I even served on a statewide access committee. When I was on that committee I met a lot of people with different disabilities, and I began to really understand the rationale behind the access rules. In the end, we tried to incorporate as many access features as we could into our historic property."

Today the Harraseeket Inn includes two accessible guest rooms. Room 107 is located on the ground floor and features a level entry, wide doorways, good pathway access, lever handles, and a lowered closet rod. The bathroom has a tub/shower combination with a hand-held shower, a roll-under sink, and grab bars in the toilet and shower areas. There is a full five-foot turning radius in the spacious bathroom, and a shower chair is available upon request. Room 204 has these same access features, except it has a roll-in shower in place of the tub/shower combination.

Room 107 at the Harraseeket Inn is located on the ground floor and features good pathway access.

There is good access throughout the public areas of the inn, including the two on-site restaurants. And this is one of the few inns where I have ever seen *New Mobility* and other disability publications in the magazine rack.

Nightly room rates in the high season (July 1 to October 31) range from $195 to $275. The bargain season is from mid-May to July 1, when the weather is still quite mild, and the room rates are $160 to $235 per night.

You just can't beat the location of the Harraseeket Inn, as it's only a few blocks away from the hundreds of outlets that line Freeport's main drag. Access is fairly good in downtown Freeport. This pedestrian-friendly town has wide sidewalks and plentiful curb-cuts. About 75% of the shops have level entries and access to at least one floor. Many of the shops are housed in historic buildings and have a few steps or narrow doorways, but there are still plenty of accessible shopping choices in the downtown area.

If you'd prefer to enjoy the great outdoors, head on over to Wolf Neck Woods State Park, where you'll find the accessible White Pines Trail. This hard-packed dirt trail winds through the forest and alongside the Harraseeket River. It is four feet wide, level, and very easy to navigate in a wheelchair or scooter. Says Chip, "It's one of the few accessible trails in the area that actually takes you right down to the water."

If you visit during the late spring, be on the lookout for lady's slippers in the shady areas on the forest floor. These pink orchids are a protected species in Maine, and they bloom from late May to early July. And no matter when you go, don't forget the insect repellent!

Harraseeket Inn
162 Main Street
Freeport, Maine 04032
(207) 865-9377
www.harraseeketinn.com

Waterloo Country Inn

*I*nnkeeper Theresa Kraemer describes her Waterloo Country Inn as a luxurious pre-Revolutionary waterfront estate. Built in the 1750s by prominent Somerset County landowner Henry Waggaman, this historic mansion was lovingly restored in 1995. During the extensive renovation, access features were added to the inn. Today the Waterloo Country Inn not only contains personal touches from Theresa's native Switzerland, it also has a wheelchair-accessible guest room.

Access to this historic mansion is good, with a barrier-free pathway to the inn and level access to the house. The accessible ground-floor Manokin Room features a king-sized bed that can be converted to two twin beds. There is plenty of room to maneuver a wheelchair in this spacious suite. The bathroom has a tub/shower combination with a hand-held shower, a roll-under sink, and grab bars in the shower and around the toilet.

The rest of the ground-floor public rooms, including the dining room, the lounge, and the library, all feature barrier-free access.

Nightly rates for the Manokin Room range from $105 in the off season to $145 in the peak season. The peak season runs from May to October.

The inn is situated on a tidal pond, and it's a perfect spot for bird-watchers and nature-lovers. There are wide, level trails along nearby Monie Creek, where you can roll around and explore the great outdoors.

In short, this property offers the best of two worlds, as it's nestled in a rural setting but is just a short distance away from the sandy beaches of Ocean City, Chincoteague, and the Assateague Islands. Theresa recommends visiting the historic towns of Princess Anne, Snow Hill, and Berlin. It's a beautiful drive and there are many local antique shops that are worth a stop, even if you don't buy anything.

Waterloo Country Inn
28822 Mt. Vernon Road
Princess Anne, MD 21853
(410) 651-0883
www.waterloocountryinn.com

Whale Walk Inn

EASTHAM, MASSACHUSETTS

T ucked away on a secluded Cape Cod country road, the Whale Walk Inn is situated on three beautiful acres filled with manicured lawns, meadowlands, and wildflowers. Located on the quieter side of the cape, this former sea captain's home was originally constructed in the 1830s, and was later renovated and converted to a romantic 16-room B&B.

Elaine and Kevin Conlin, the fifth owners of the inn, purchased it in 2001. Says Elaine, "Access was one of the features we looked for when we were shopping for an inn. We learned about the importance of having an accessible property when we took a B&B course prior to purchasing the inn."

The Whale Walk Inn is made up of five buildings that date from 1830 to 1897, and although the main house has steps at the entrance, there is a nicely accessible room located in the detached carriage house. It features ramped access and is simply called Carriage House 1.

Carriage House 1 features a four-poster queen-sized bed, a gas fireplace, and a refrigerator. This spacious ground-floor room has wide doorways and good pathway access. The bathroom has a roll-in shower, grab bars in the shower and around the toilet, and a roll-under sink. The room also has level access to a private patio that overlooks the adjacent meadow.

Breakfast is traditionally served in the dining room in the main house, but other arrangements can be made for people who cannot manage the steps into the house. Says Elaine, "We're happy to deliver breakfast to the room, or help in any other way we can."

The nightly rate for Carriage House 1 ranges from $205 to $225. This rate includes a full breakfast, cookies in the afternoon, and an hors d'oeuvres hour in the evening.

The inn is located in the unhurried part of Cape Cod, yet it's still close to all of the popular tourist attractions. As far as accessible activities go, Elaine recommends checking out the Cape Cod Rail Trail, which runs right behind the inn. Says Elaine, "This accessible trail was once an old railroad bed, and it traverses 30 miles through beautiful salt marshes, water kettle ponds, state parks, and small village hamlets. It's a great place to enjoy the unspoiled environment of outer Cape Cod."

The inn is also just a 10-minute drive from the Cape Cod National Seashore, where you will find several more accessible nature trails. And If you really want to hit the beach, head over to Coast Guard Beach in Eastham or Herring Cove Beach in Provincetown, where you will find beach wheelchairs available for free loan. They're great fun and a good way to get around on the beach.

Whale Walk Inn
220 Bridge Road
Eastham, MA 02642
(508) 255-0617
www.whalewalkinn.com

The Allen House

SCITUATE, MASSACHUSETTS

*B*uilt in 1905 by William Paley Allen, the Allen House is located 25 miles southeast of Boston in the charming fishing village of Scituate. This shingle-style colonial house sits high on a hill and overlooks the harbor, which is just 250 yards away.

Innkeeper Meredith Emmons purchased the inn in January 2000, and spent the next four months restoring the property before reopening it in May. Although the access features were already in place when Meredith bought the property, she did her best to make sure that her other improvements did not impede the existing access. Her efforts paid off, as today this six-room inn offers wheelchair-users and slow walkers a nicely accessible (yet historic) lodging option.

Although there are seven steps at the front entrance of the inn, there is also a ramp that leads up to the front door. Accessible parking is located near the base of the ramp, and a barrier-free path leads from the ramp to the paved parking area. The front door is 40" wide, and although there is a slight lip at the threshold, it's really quite doable for most wheelchair-users. The accessible Harbor View Room is located on the first floor.

The Harbor View Room features a king-sized bed, a gas log stove, and great town and harbor views. Access features include wide doorways and good pathway access. This spacious guest room measures 217 square feet and the bathroom measure 65.6 square feet. It's important to note that there is a sharp right turn near the entrance; however, there is also a full 37" of clearance space in this area.

The bathroom features a roll-in shower with a hand-held showerhead, a roll-under sink and a lowered swivel mirror. A portable shower chair is available upon request.

A buffet breakfast is served in the first-floor dining room. There is barrier-free access to the dining room through two pocket doors at the entrance. The staff is happy to provide assistance with the buffet, or to deliver breakfast to your room upon request. Says Emmons, "We are very flexible and do what we can to assist. With advance notice, we also cater to lactose-intolerant, diabetic or vegetarian diets."

All of the first-floor public rooms, including the foyer, living room, reading room, and porch, have barrier-free access.

Nightly rates for the Harbor View Room range from $165 to $195.

As far as accessible sightseeing goes, Emmons recommends Plymouth Plantation or the National Historic Park in Quincy. "Plymouth Plantation is 22 miles away, and it is partially wheelchair-accessible," she says. "If you have a power wheelchair it is fully accessible," she adds, "as the village is very hilly." The National Historic Park in Quincy is 21.5 miles away, and it is also partially wheelchair-accessible.

Locally, Emmons recommends the accessible Mill Wharf Restaurant. "It's right on the water and they have a ramp at the front entrance and elevator access to the second floor. The outside decks also have ramp access."

To be honest, Emmons adds, "Most people stay here for events like weddings, reunions, or anniversaries. Scituate is a favorite pick for people just looking to get away from the hustle and bustle of the city.

The Allen House
18 Allen Place
Scituate, MA 02066
(781) 545-8221
www.allenhousebnb.com

Stone Mill Suites

LANESBORO, MINNESOTA

*B*uilt in 1885, the building that now houses Stone Mill Suites has served many purposes over its lifetime. This limestone building has been a cold storage facility, an egg and poultry processing plant, and a feed storage facility. Finally, in October 1999, the Lamon-Mortimer family purchased the building and began an extensive restoration project.

Says innkeeper Colleen Mortimer, "We managed to preserve most of the building's historic structure while adding some modern touches. All of our rooms have a microwave, refrigerator, television, and a coffeemaker. The local building code dictated that we have an accessible room, but I thought it was a good idea regardless of the rules."

The Mortimer's welcomed their first guests to Stone Mill Suites on July 13, 2001. Says Colleen, "From the beginning, our goal has been to provide a fun lodging experience for all of our guests."

Stone Mill Suites features 10 themed guest rooms that focus on the history of the building and the charm of the local area. There is ramp access to the front entrance of the inn, with accessible parking at the foot of the ramp. The accessible Boat Suite is located on the first floor.

The Boat Suite highlights the many ways people can travel down the nearby Root River. It is decorated with boat-shaped shelves and nature collectibles. Access features include wide doorways and good pathway access.

The bathroom features a five-foot turning radius and a roll-in shower with a hand-held showerhead and a fold-down shower seat. There are grab bars in the shower and around the toilet. There is also a standard two-person Jacuzzi tub in the suite.

The Fishing Room, which is located on the first floor, is also worth a mention. This room does not have any access adaptations, but it's a good choice for slow walkers who cannot manage the stairs to the second floor rooms. It's important to note that this room has a standard tub/shower combination, and it does not have grab bars or any other access features. This room is not appropriate for wheelchair-users.

There is barrier-free access to the first-floor breakfast room. Adds Colleen, "There is always someone on staff at the desk during breakfast, and they are willing to lend a hand whenever needed."

The nightly rates for the Boat Suite range from $100 to $140. The Fishing Room rents for $80 to $120 per night.

Says Colleen, "In the summer, spring, and fall our guests enjoy sitting on our deck and just taking in the serenity of the whole area. The deck is ramped, so it's perfect for wheelchair-users and slow walkers. Everybody can enjoy the great view!"

Stone Mill Suites
100 Beacon Street East
Lanesboro, MN 55949
(507) 467-8663
www.stonemillsuites.com

Loon Song B&B

*L*oon Song B&B is located on the shores of Lake Heart, just 35 minutes north of Park Rapids and six miles from Itasca State Park. The home was originally constructed by David and Joyce Johnson, who thought of it as their retirement dream.

Says David, "This was our home as well as a B&B, so we made sure to include accessible features in it. We are both over 65 years old, and we thought it was a good idea to make it accessible, just in case we would need it in the future. Also, we wanted to be able to share this wonderful setting with everybody."

In 2004, innkeepers Barb and Dennis Cowan purchased the property, and they are equally enthusiastic about sharing their home with all travelers. Barb is very proud of the access at her B&B, and she truly understands the need for more accessible lodging options. Says Barb, "We've had a number of wheelchair-users stay with us, and they've all made comments about the good access of the Garden Room."

The accessible Garden Room is located on the first floor. It features a queen-sized bed, a private entrance, and a small patio. There is level access to the front door, and accessible parking is located approximately 15 feet from the front entry. Access features include wide doorways and good pathway access throughout the room.

The bathroom has a five-foot turning radius, a roll-under sink and a low-step shower with a hand-held showerhead and a built-in shower bench. There is a six-inch lip on the shower, and there are grab bars in the shower and around the toilet. Even though the shower threshold is not flush, it's still possible to transfer to the shower bench.

There is barrier-free access to all of the first-floor public rooms, including the dining room, the reading room, and the all-season porch. There are level sidewalks around the building and through the garden, while the beach and dock are accessible by an 80' packed gravel path.

Nightly rates for the Garden Room range from $75 to $99. Rates vary depending on the season, the day of the week, and the length of the stay.

Accessible attractions in the area include Itasca State Park, the Mississippi River Wilderness Drive, and Douglas Lodge.

Adds Barb, "Our inn is very secluded and quiet. We are located three miles from the nearest paved road. There is no traffic noise, no airplane noise, and almost no boating activity on our lake. It's a very peaceful place. That's what our guests love most about our B&B."

Loon Song B&B
17248 Loonsong Lane
Park Rapids, MN 56470
(218) 266-3333
www.loonsongbedandbreakfast.com

Hermann Inns

HERMANN, MISSOURI

*N*estled along the banks of the Missouri River, just 90 minutes from downtown Saint Louis, lies the quaint town of Hermann. Granted, it's a bit off the beaten path, but that's part of the attraction of this picturesque German village. It's also located in the heart of Missouri wine country and near a major trailhead of the very accessible Katy Trail.

It's a treat to even find one accessible property in a small town, but we hit the jackpot in Hermann and came away with two choices. The Captain Wohlt Inn is located in the middle of the historic district, while the Hermann Hill Inn is situated on a hillside vineyard. Both offer different levels of access, but either one makes a great base for exploring this scenic area.

Named for a local steamer captain, the Captain Wohlt Inn spans four buildings and has five guest rooms, including the accessible Sweetheart Room. Innkeeper Kent Wilkins purchased the property in Feburary 2001 when he relocated to Hermann.

Says Wilkins, "When we bought the Captain Wohlt Inn, the Sweetheart Room was listed as 'wheelchair accessible.' We have changed a few things to make it more friendly, and we have so thoroughly enjoyed our guests who have needed it that we would truly like to make more of our facility accessible."

The inn is located in an alley between 2nd Street and 3rd Street, and there is a large parking lot right beside it. The most accessible entrance to the main building (which houses the Sweetheart Room) is located near the parking lot on the alley side of the inn. This entrance is ramped, and there is a wide cement walkway from the accessible parking space to the alley entrance.

The first-floor Sweetheart Room features wide doorways, a queen-sized bed, and plenty of room to maneuver a wheelchair. Says Wilkins, "Since the bed is a little high, we also have a rollaway bed available for guests who want or need it. Even with the rollaway bed set up there is still plenty of floor space in the room." The room also has two sturdy armchairs that were added at the suggestion of a former guest.

The oversized bathroom features a raised toilet and a tub/shower combination with standard controls. "We also have a sturdy, screw-on grab bar, which we install before a guest needing it arrives," adds Wilkins.

All of the first-floor public rooms, including the dining room and the kitchen, feature wide doorways and barrier-free access. The outside areas are equally inviting, and there is level access to the patio.

The nightly rates for the Sweetheart Room are $70 during the week and $85 on weekends.

Located across the river from the Katy Trail, the eight-room Hermann Hill Inn was built in 1995. It includes one wheelchair-accessible guest room, Chambourcin. Says innkeeper Terry Hammer, "We're continuing to work on our accessibility, and right now we are trying to figure out how to make another guest room accessible."

Because of the unique construction of this hillside property, the main entrance is located on the third floor. This level entrance is approximately 75' from the accessible parking area. There is elevator access to the second floor, where Chambourcin is located. There is also a private entrance to this room that can be reached via a sidewalk from the parking area. Says Hammer, "In the event of electrical or elevator failure, the private entrance is always available."

Chambourcin features wide doorways, lever hardware, and good pathway access. The bathroom has a roll-in shower with a hand-held showerhead and a fold-down shower seat. There is also a separate (non-accessible) Jacuzzi tub. The toilet has grab bars on one side and along the back wall. One of the unique features of Chambourcin is the private patio that borders a vineyard. The patio features level access, and it's the perfect place to enjoy breakfast.

Breakfast can also be served in the kitchen, the dining room, or on the deck, all of which are wheelchair-accessible.

The nightly rates for Chambourcin range from $140 to $295. The lowest rates are available midweek from January to March.

The Katy Trail tops the list of accessible area activities. This multi-use trail runs from Clinton to St. Charles, along the abandoned rail bed of the former Missouri–Kansas–Texas Railroad. It offers a great opportunity for wheelers and slow walkers to explore Missouri's natural side, as the grade rarely exceeds 5% and the surface is covered with crushed limestone. Indeed, it's very rollable.

"There are also many wineries in our area," adds Hammer. "Stone Hill is the largest, and it has dining, wine-tasting, and a large gift shop. Many of our guests like to go wine-tasting."

The Captain Wohlt Inn
123 East Third Street
Hermann, MO 65041
(573) 486-3357
www.captainwohltbandb.com

The Hermann Hill Inn
711 Wein Street
Hermann, MO 65041
(573) 486-4455
www.hermannhill.com

Kansas City Picks

*L*ocated in heart of Kansas City's historic arts, entertainment, and shopping district, Southmoreland on the Plaza features 12 luxury rooms and a separate Carriage House Suite. The previous owners were inspired to make this 1913 Colonial Revival mansion accessible due to their friendship with a woman who used a wheelchair because of post-polio syndrome.

Nancy and Mark Reichle purchased the property in December 1998. Says Nancy, "The woman who inspired the accessibility upgrades was on the board of directors of Whole Person, a local nonprofit disability advocacy group. Whole Person supervised the design of the accessible August Meyer Room and the access upgrades to the entrance and the first floor."

Accessible parking is located about 15' from the ramped side entrance of the inn.

The first-floor August Meyer Room is decorated with Civil War–era furnishings and can be configured with either two twin beds or one king-sized bed. Access features include wide doorways and adequate pathway access. The bathroom has a tub/shower combination and grab bars in the shower and around the toilet. A portable shower bench is also available.

All of the first-floor public rooms feature level access, with the exception of the solarium, which can be accessed by a portable ramp. Breakfast is generally served in the Harvest Dining Room, which is just 15' from the August Meyer Room. Alternatively, guests can enjoy breakfast on the veranda, which can be accessed by a portable ramp.

The nightly rate for the August Meyer Room is $185 year round.

Nearby accessible attractions include the American Jazz Museum, the Negro League Baseball Museum, the Nelson-Atkins Museum of Art, and the Kemper Museum of Contemporary Art. Also worth a visit is the Truman Presidential Museum & Library, located a short drive away in Independence.

In contrast to the urban setting of Southmoreland on the Plaza, the Inn on Crescent Lake is located in a more rural location, just 30 miles northeast of Kansas City. Billed as an "oasis of rest," this former estate home was converted to a 10-room inn by the previous owners. The conversion included the addition of the accessible Garden Room.

Ed and Irene Heege purchased the property in 2005. "When we saw the Inn, we thought it was gorgeous," says Irene. "We visited over twenty inns for sale and there was just no comparison."

The most accessible entrance to the inn is the ramped entrance in the back of the property. This private entrance leads directly to the Garden Room.

The Garden Room features a private deck, a queen-sized bed and a sitting area. There is level access to the deck and entrance, wide doorways and good pathway access in the room. The bathroom has a roll-in shower with a small lip and a built-in shower bench. There are grab bars in the shower and around the toilet.

All of the first-floor public rooms feature level thresholds and wide doorways. Breakfast is served in the dining room, which is just around the corner from the Garden Room.

The nightly rate for the Garden Room is $150 during the week and $165 on weekends.

Nancy is quick to point out that most of their guests come to rest and relax on the 22-acre estate, although she admits some folks take day trips into nearby Kansas City. "To be honest," she adds, "many guests prefer to just wander the property on some of our paths that lead to nowhere. It's a very relaxing atmosphere."

Southmoreland on the Plaza
116 East 46th Street
Kansas City, MO 64112
(816) 531-7979
www.southmoreland.com

The Inn On Crescent Lake
1261 St. Louis Avenue
Excelsior Springs, MO 64024
(816) 630-6745
www.crescentlake.com

The Inn at Harbour Ridge

OSAGE BEACH, MISSOURI

The Inn at Harbour Ridge is located in Central Missouri, halfway between Kansas City and St. Louis on the Lake of the Ozarks. Built in 2000, this Osage Beach inn is located in a parklike setting on a ridge above the lake. Says innkeeper Sue Westenhaver, "The peace and quiet is just wonderful up here."

Sue retired early from a 25-year banking career in order to be a full-time innkeeper. "My experience as a human resources director really prepared me for my second career as an innkeeper," she says. Considering her professional background, it's no surprise that Sue has some strong opinions about access. "I believe that everyone should be treated equally and should be able to enjoy their R & R time to the fullest," she says.

It's also no surprise that Sue and Ron included the accessible Captain's Quarters guest room when they built their inn. "Actually," Sue says, "we prefer to call it our 'special needs' guest room, as this is the term our friends with a special needs child use."

There is ramp access to the front porch (and the front door) from the side of the inn. The porch runs the width of the house, and it's a great place for bird-watching or sunset-viewing (two favorite activities at the inn).

The Captain's Quarters room is located on the first floor, and it has a king-sized bed, wide doorways, and plenty of room to maneuver a wheelchair. The bathroom has a roll-in shower (with a small lip) and a built-in shower seat, grab bars in the shower, a roll-under sink, and a raised toilet. There are no grab bars by the toilet, but there is a walker in the closet to help with transfers. The room also has a private deck with ramp access, which is a great place to enjoy breakfast or cocktails.

All of the first-floor public rooms are wheelchair-accessible, including the common area, the screened porch, the dining room, and the kitchen. The open floor plan makes it very easy for wheelchair-users to move from one room to the next.

The nightly rate for the Captain's Quarters room is $149.

Of course the lake is the big draw in the area, and the inn is located just five minutes from Public Beach 2. "Shopping is another favorite pastime of our guests," adds Sue. "There are 110 stores at the Outlet Mall and most of those shops are accessible, as are most of our specialty and antique shops. We also have some great accessible dining options here."

The Inn at Harbour Ridge
6334 Red Barn Road
Osage Beach, MO 65065
(573) 302-0411
www.harbourridgeinn.com

The Walnut Street Inn

T he Walnut Street Inn is located in the heart of Springfield, just one block from historic Route 66. This Queen Anne–style Victorian inn features 12 guest rooms: six in the main house, four in the carriage house, and two in the cottage house. Formerly known as the McCann-Jewell House, this historic property was converted to a B&B in 1988. In fact, the Walnut Street Inn was Springfield's very first B&B.

Innkeepers Gary and Paula Blankenship purchased the property in 1996. Says Gary, "Fortunately, when we purchased the inn all of the accessible areas were already set. The previous owners built in the access features when they converted the property to a B&B."

Although the front entrance of the inn has steps, there is ramp access from the parking lot to the back entrance. Says Gary, "Most of our guests prefer to come and go from the back entrance anyway because it's closer to the parking." The accessible parking area is approximately 30 yards away from the back entrance behind some of the outbuildings. Says Gary, "Most of our disabled guests prefer to park in the back lot instead of the accessible parking area. There's always plenty of room there and it's closer to the back door."

The accessible Jewell Room is located on the first floor of Carriage House, which is right behind the main house. It features a level threshold, wide doorways, and a queen-sized canopy bed. The bathroom has a tub/shower combination and a roll-under sink. A portable shower bench and a hand-held shower are available upon request.

Breakfast can either be served in the Jewell Room (at a table next to the fireplace) or in the dining room in the main house. All of the first-floor public areas of the main house are wheelchair-accessible. This includes the parlor, dining room and the back deck.

The nightly rate for the Jewell Room is $169.

The Springfield area offers a wide variety of accessible diversions, including the very popular Bass Pro Shop. This enormous sportsman's outlet features a wide selection of hunting, fishing, and camping gear at very attractive prices. In fact, people come from all over the U.S. just to shop at this store.

If shopping isn't your cup of tea, then head on over to Exotic Animal Paradise. Located just 12 miles east of Springfield, this drive-through wild animal park is home to over 3,000 animals, including deer, elk, llamas, rheas and buffaloes. It's very accessible as you feed the animals from the comfort and safety of your own car. It's also great fun.

And If you really want to try something unique, check out Fantastic Caverns. Cavern tours are conducted in a ramped tram, and wheelers can stay in their own wheelchair for the duration of the 55-minute narrated tour. The tram follows an ancient riverbed and gives visitors a great look at some of the magnificent stalactite and stalagmite formations in the cave.

There are lots of things to do in and around Springfield. Says Gary, "We are a fun place to stay in the heart of a wonderful city!"

The Walnut Street Inn
900 East Walnut Street
Springfield, MO 65806
(417) 864-6346
www.walnutstreetinn.com

Fantastic Caverns offers roll–on access to their tram cave tours.

The Lodge at Grant's Trail

ST. LOUIS, MISSOURI

*L*ocated just 10 minutes south of the famous St. Louis Gateway Arch, The Lodge at Grant's Trail offers guests the best of both worlds; casual luxury in a rustic setting. This semi-rural property features eight uniquely designed guest rooms, including the accessible Christmas Room.

As the owners of Orlando's Catering and Orlando Gardens Banquet and Conference Centers, the proprietors of The Lodge at Grant's Trail realized the importance of making their property accessible from the beginning. Says innkeeper Jan Orlando, "The need for all people to enjoy the availability of a B&B atmosphere seems only fair. Sadly, many B&Bs are in existing older homes that aren't accessible to wheelchair-users. We wanted our lodge to be accessible to everybody."

In keeping with that proactive attitude, access was built into The Lodge at Grant's Trail from the ground up. When the Orlandos welcomed their first guests in July 2000, their three-story log cabin lodge was truly accessible to everyone.

The good access starts before you ever enter the lodge, with accessible parking located near the ramped front entrance. Because of the unique construction of the building, guests actually enter the lodge on the second floor. Alternatively you can drive around the building and enter the first-floor great room and use the elevator to travel between the first and second floors.

The accessible Christmas Room is located near the entrance on the second floor. The name appropriately describes the decor, as a bevy of Christmas ornaments, pillows, photos, and even some slippers decorate this festive room. A corner fireplace completes the cozy holiday setting.

Access features include wide doorways and wheelchair-access to one side of the bed. Access to the private bathroom is by a large pocket door.

The Lodge at Grant's Trail features ramped access from the parking lot.

The bathroom, which is also decorated in a Christmas motif, features a full five-foot turning radius and a tub/shower combination with grab bars and a hand-held shower. Other access features include a roll-under sink, a lowered mirror, lever hardware, and grab bars by the toilet. It's very nicely done, with some unique touches such as dual showerheads and a fold-down wooden bath bench.

All of the second- and third-floor public areas are accessible, including the great room, the first-floor patio, and the Lewis & Clark Sitting Room. Breakfast is served downstairs, next to the fireplace in the great room. Wine and cheese is served in the afternoon, either in your room or in the great room.

Nightly rates for the Christmas Room range from $100 on weeknights to $129 on the weekends.

The lodge gets its name from the Ulysses S. Grant Trail, which runs behind the property. Leased and operated by St. Louis County Parks, this Rails to Trails conversion was constructed along an old railroad corridor in 1997.

The first six miles of the trail are paved. This portion of the trail has a wide, level surface that is ideal for wheeling. The trail actually begins at the parking area below the lodge and ends at Grant's Farm, eight miles away.

The portion of the trail near the lodge is partially shaded by the surrounding trees, and it makes for a very pleasant walk, even on hot summer days. As an added treat, there is a snowcone stand about a mile down the trail.

Although it's quite a hike to Grant's Farm, it's just a few minutes away by car and definitely worth a visit. Originally farmed by Ulysses S. Grant (hence the name "Grant's Farm") this land later became the ancestral home of the Anheuser-Busch family. In keeping with their commitment to animal conservation, the Busch family later converted the land to a wildlife preserve and opened it to the public.

Today visitors can board a tram and tour the 281-acre deer park; home to a large variety of deer, antelope, zebras, elk, and bison. The first car of the tram features ramp access with room for two wheelchairs. The tram stops at the Tier Garden and the Bauerhof before it returns to the main entrance. Visitors can visit the Tier Garden to feed the animals, or stop by the Bauerhof to see the carriage collection. There are a few steep grades along the asphalt paths in the Tier Garden, but wheelchair-users can still get an up-close-and-personal look at the majority of the animals.

Guests can also enjoy a free sample of their favorite Anheuser-Busch adult beverage. And don't forget to visit the famous Clydesdales! Grant's Farm is open from April to October, and admission is free.

The Lodge at Grant's Trail
4398 Hoffmeister Avenue
St. Louis, MO 63125
(314) 638-3340
www.lodgeatgrantstrail.com

Roaring Lion Inn

HAMILTON, MONTANA

*L*ocated in the heart of Montana's Bitterroot Valley, the three-room Roaring Lion Inn was constructed in 1999 by wheelchair-user Lee Goldstein. As the former innkeeper, Lee needed access to all areas of the property, so he designed the property to be accessible to him.

The current owners, Gregg and Suzanne Couch, purchased the property in 2001. Suzanne visited the area on several vacations and just fell in love with the natural beauty of the Bitterroot Valley. Says Susan, "This property is just ideal for slow walkers, as there are level pathways all around it. We had a senior group here for lunch last month and they just loved the fact that there is level access to the inn and the dining room."

Although all the guest rooms at the Roaring Lion Inn feature wide doorways and level thresholds, the most accessible choice is the Montanan Room. This western-style room features a king-sized bed, a leather sleeper sofa, wood floors, a mini refrigerator, and a microwave oven. It is the largest guest room in the inn, and it also has an accessible private entrance. Access features in the bathroom include a roll-in shower, a roll-under sink, and grab bars by the toilet and in the shower. There is also a separate Jacuzzi tub in the bathroom.

It should be noted that because of the bed and toilet height, this room may not work for some full-time wheelchair-users; however, the Couches are willing to do whatever they can to make things as accessible as possible. Says Suzanne, "We removed the box spring for one gentleman to lower the bed, but we've had other disabled guests who said the height was just fine for them. And several guests who use a cane just loved our roll-in shower."

The two other guest rooms, the Bitterroot Room and the Selway Room, have wide doorways and good pathway access, but they do not have any bathroom adaptations.

Wooden floors, wide doorways and accessible pathways are found throughout the inn. All of the public spaces, including the dining room and the great room, feature barrier-free access.

The nightly rate for the Montanan Room is $150. The Bitterroot Room rents for $115 per night, and the Selway Room rents for $135 per night.

There are accessible pathways around the property and at nearby Lake Como. Says Suzanne, "Binocular hunting and photography are popular activities for many of our guests. The wildlife in this area is abundant and it includes everything from elk, bears and moose to porcupines, beavers and bald eagles, many of which have been spotted from our front porch!"

Roaring Lion Inn
830 Timberbrook Lane
Hamilton, MT 59840
(406) 363-6555
www.roaringlioninn.com

Cabernet Inn

The 11-room Cabernet Inn was constructed in 1842 and it served its first life as a Victorian cottage. As with many historic buildings it has been upgraded and retrofitted many times over the years. The most recent upgrades were added in 1992, when the property was converted to an inn and accessible features were added.

Today the Cabernet Inn reflects the elegance of the past and comfort and amenities of the present. Although the access upgrades were in place when the current owners purchased the property, Jessica and Bruce Zarenko admit they continue to be a big hit with their guests.

The accessible Harvest Moon Room is located on the ground floor and features a queen-sized bed, a gas fireplace, and a two-person (non-accessible) Jacuzzi tub. This premium room is a top honeymoon choice; indeed, it's the perfect venue for any romantic getaway.

Access features include wide doorways, good pathway access, a roll-in shower, a roll-under sink, and grab bars in the shower and around the toilet. Accessible parking is available right outside the room. As an added bonus, there is level access to a private brick patio, which is the perfect place to enjoy a quiet breakfast.

The innkeepers have received many compliments on the Harvest Moon Room over the years, but the most memorable one came from a British woman who visited the inn with her wheeler husband. When she saw the room and the Jacuzzi she tearfully exclaimed, "This is the first time that I've ever had an accessible room with a Jacuzzi tub. I'm so happy there is something here for me too."

The ground-floor gathering room features level access, but there are three steps up to the dining room. Outside there is good pathway access to the beautiful perennial gardens, and there are over 40 miles of groomed cross-country skiing trails behind the inn. Most of these trails are easily navigable in a wheelchair during the summer months.

The nightly rate for the Harvest Moon Room ranges from $145 to $225, depending on the season.

The innkeepers have plenty of sightseeing suggestions. "Skiing, hiking, and shopping are the big attractions in this area, but we also have the Mt. Washington Auto Road, a very scenic drive with some tremendous views. As long as the car you are in is accessible, so is the Mt. Washington Auto Road."

Cabernet Inn
3552 White Mountain Highway
North Conway, NH 03860
(603) 356-4704
www.cabernetinn.com

Inn of the
Tartan Fox

SWANZEY, NEW HAMPSHIRE

B uilt in 1832, the Inn of the Tartan Fox is a four-room B&B located near Keene, New Hampshire. Formerly a large homestead named Meademere, the property was purchased by innkeepers Wayne Miller and Meg Kupiec in 1998. Over the next year they worked hard to convert this stately Arts-and-Crafts style house to a B&B.

Says Wayne, "When we renovated the house we paid particular attention to making the downstairs room fully accessible. We have a friend who needs accessibility, and we felt that this was something that most B&Bs didn't offer.

"As it worked out, because of the layout of the house, one guest room had to be located on the first floor," Wayne continues. "We realized this presented us with the perfect opportunity to create an accessible room, so we asked our wheelchair-using friend to make some access suggestions. The result is the very accessible Terrace Room."

Entry to the Terrace Room is through French doors from the patio or via the 36" hallway door. A brick covered ramp leads up to the patio. The private pergola-covered patio is covered with wisteria blossoms in the spring and trumpet vine blooms all summer long. There are no steps to the adjacent screen porch.

The Terrace Room has a queen-sized bed, hardwood floors, a fireplace, and a bathroom with a heated marble floor. The bathroom has a five-foot turning radius, a roll-in shower, and a raised toilet.

Says Wayne, "The wheelchair guests that have stayed with us said they love the Terrace Room because it fits so well into the rest of the house without disturbing the turn-of-the-century feel."

The grounds are filled with flowers, gardens, and ponds. The bridge across the ponds can be accessed in a wheelchair. The public areas, includ-

The Terrace Room at the Inn of the Tartan Fox features a spacious bathroom with a roll-in shower. (Photo courtesy of the Inn of the Tartan Fox.)

ing a large common room, hallway, breakfast room, and gift shop, all have hardwood floors and good pathway access. The small sun porch is accessible from the exterior, but there are two steps from the breakfast room to the sun porch.

The rates for the Terrace Room range from $100 to $120 per night.

Wayne's sightseeing suggestions include the six covered bridges in the area, antique shops, country auctions, old book stores, and the world-famous Keene Pumpkinfest. Adds Wayne, "Downtown Keene is an attraction by itself, and the nearby Rhododendron State Park has some wheelable paths. There are really a lot of things to see and do in this area."

Inn of the Tartan Fox
350 Old Homestead Highway
Swanzey, NH 03446
(603) 357-9308
www.tartanfox.com

Colonnade Inn

*D*uring the 1890s the Colonnade Inn was one of the smaller hotels in the popular seaside resort town of Sea Isle City. Over 100 years later Dr. Carolyn Crawford purchased the property, restored it and furnished it with Victorian antiques. Indeed her love of the Victorian era is evident throughout the refurbished house. Dr. Crawford welcomed her first guests to the newly restored property in 1991. Today the Colonnade Inn still makes a great seaside getaway, as it combines the charm of the past with the comforts of the present.

Even though the property was restored in pre-ADA times, Dr. Crawford took care to make the property as accessible as possible. She understands the need for accessible lodging options because she knows many people with disabilities, including her former husband.

Says innkeeper Deedra Cavella, "When Dr. Crawford was originally researching the city, many real estate agents expressed their concerns about the lack of accessible accommodations. Dr. Crawford felt this shortage was very unfortunate, so when she renovated the property she converted one of the ground-floor rooms to a wheelchair-accessible suite. She felt it was natural fit, considering the size and location of the room."

The accessible Mansfield Executive Suite features ramped access, wide doorways, and adequate room to navigate in a wheelchair or scooter. This three-bedroom suite includes a private bathroom with a roll-in shower and a (non-accessible) whirlpool tub. There is also a fully equipped kitchen and a large living room in the suite. Deedra adds, "With advance notice, guests can also arrange to have a hospital bed delivered to the suite."

The Devonshire Suite and Chelsea Suite, which are located on the ground floor, may also work for some slow walkers who cannot climb the stairs to the second floor. They feature wide doorways and good pathway access, but they do not have roll-in showers.

Most of the public spaces, including the breakfast room and the parlor area, feature level access, although some furniture may have to be moved to accommodate wheelchair-users. Outdoor amenities include a small garden area that is accessible from the sidewalk.

Nightly rates at the Colonnade Inn range from $88 to $280. The rates vary by season, and guests are encouraged to call for the best available rate.

Local attractions include an accessible beach boardwalk lined with shops and restaurants. Deedra also reminds visitors, "Cape May is just 30 minutes away." The Cape May–Lewes Ferry is nicely accessible, thanks to a recent $54.4-million capital renovation project. The five vessels feature elevators, threshold ramps, accessible bathrooms, and automatic doors. It's a fun cruise and it makes a great day trip.

Colonnade Inn
4600 Landis Avenue
Sea Isle City, NJ 08243
(609) 263-0460
www.colonnadeinn.com

Hacienda Manzanal

*L*ocated in a rural farming community just outside Albuquerque, Hacienda Manzanal blends in perfectly with the surrounding landscape. Says innkeeper Sue Gregory, "Manzanal means 'apple orchard' in Spanish; and that's what was here before we built the house—an apple orchard." Indeed, a few apple trees still remain today. Combine that with the horses next door, a quiet country lane, and a very hospitable innkeeper, and you can begin to understand the attraction of this very relaxed suburban property. In short, it's a little bit country.

Constructed in 1991, the hacienda-style inn features wide doorways, level access, and barrier-free pathways throughout the first floor. Parking is located close to entrance in a crushed gravel parking lot. And when it came time to design the accessible El Rancho Grande Room, Sue got a little help from a friend.

Says Sue, "I have a very good friend with arthritis, and she will eventually be in a wheelchair. She has plans to move to Texas, and when she comes back to visit I want to be able to accommodate her, so she helped me set up the accessible guest room in her favorite Western theme."

The spacious first-floor El Rancho Grande Room features wide doorways, a corner fireplace, and a walk-in closet with lowered closet rods. The tiled bathroom has a full five-foot turning radius, a roll-in shower with a hand-held showerhead, grab bars in the shower, and a roll-under sink. A portable shower chair and a toilet riser with attached grab bars are also available upon request.

All of the public areas, including the dining room, living room and the very pleasant verandah, feature barrier-free access.

The rate for the El Rancho Grande Room is $105 per night.

Says Sue, "The biggest attraction around Corrales is the Albuquerque International Balloon fiesta in October." And if you like scenic drives, check out the Sandia Crest Scenic Byway (NM 536), a National Scenic Byway that

Hacienda Manzanal features level access from the front parking lot and good pathway access throughout the first floor.

curves through numerous overlooks on the way to summit of Sandia Peak. Save some time to explore Elena Gallegos Picnic Area, at the Tramway exit off of I-40. This newly developed Open Space Project features a wheelchair-accessible nature trail, and it's a nice place to enjoy a picnic lunch. If you like the outdoors, there's really a lot to see in the area.

Hacienda Manzanal
300 West Meadowlark Lane
Corrales, NM 87048
(505) 922-1662
www.haciendamanzanal.com

Dream Catcher Inn

Although Anita McLeod is new to innkeeping, in a sense she's been in the hospitality business for many years. "Prior to opening our Dream Catcher Inn, we averaged about 150 nights of company every year," says Anita. "I figured if I could do that, I could manage an inn."

So Anita and her husband Ken packed up their belongings, sold their Kansas City home, and headed out west with Sam and Ken (their two cats) and Bill (their very spoiled African Grey Parrot). Their goal was to build an accessible B&B in the scenic New Mexican desert. After finding the perfect site—at the base of the Organ Mountains just outside Las Cruces—they set out to design and build their dream property, and in March 2005, they welcomed their first guests.

As the result of knee surgery and arthritis, Anita walks with a cane, so access is very important to her. "Through our travels, I've come to realize that many so-called accessible rooms are actually pretty poorly equipped," says Anita. "It's our goal to provide a beautiful property with as many access features as possible."

And they did a very good job in that respect. The Southwestern architecture of the three-room inn features wide doorways, level pathways, and no steps. Parking is conveniently located in front of the rooms, and all of the guest rooms have good pathway access, touch-control bedside lamps, lowered closet rods, tile floors, and a separate back entrance that leads out to the desert.

Room 1 and Room 2 are mirror images of each other. They each have a pocket door to the bathroom, a roll-in shower with a built-in shower seat and a hand-held showerhead, grab bars by the toilet and in the shower, a roll-under sink, and plenty of counter space. Room 1 has the toilet grab bars on the left wall (facing the toilet) and Room 2 has the grab bars on the right wall.

The tiled roll-in showers are very nicely done, with the built-in seat located near the shower controls. Anita wanted to make the rooms attractive as well as functional. Says Anita, "I really wanted to get away from that institutional feel that some accessible rooms have." She adds, "Actually we had to have the builder redo the showers because we didn't think the seats were large enough. I'm glad we did, as I'm very happy with the results."

Room 1 and Room 2 also have slightly different beds. Both are queen-sized, but the bed in Room 2 has a four-poster wooden frame that extends along the side of the bed. Because of the design of the frame, it's difficult to get a wheelchair close enough for a safe transfer. The platform bed is 29" high, so the height combined with the frame may make transfers difficult for many wheelchair-users.

Room 2 at the Dream Catcher Inn features a queen–sized four–poster bed.

Although the open-frame bed in Room 1 is actually a half-inch higher, it lacks the wooden bed frame and so it may be a better choice for wheelchair-users or for people who travel with a Hoyer lift.

Room 3 has a king-sized bed and a jet tub with grab bars. It also has good pathway access and many of the same access features as the other two rooms. The major difference is the lack of access adaptations in the bathroom. This room is best suited for somebody who needs pathway access but does not require a roll-in shower.

All of the public areas, including the lobby, dining room, and guest kitchen, feature barrier-free access. A BBQ is also available to guests, and it's very relaxing to enjoy the desert sunset while grilling your dinner on the patio. Anita is working on the landscaping and hopes to put in accessible pathways around their 10-acre property in the future.

The nightly rate for Room 1 or Room 2 is $95. Room 3 rents for $125 per night.

As for accessible sights in the area, don't miss the newly renovated interdune boardwalk at nearby White Sands National Monument. Downtown Las Cruces also offers some unique accessible attractions, such as the Branigan Cultural Center, the Museum of Fine Arts, and the Railroad Museum. And for some great deals on local crafts, don't miss the twice-weekly market in the downtown mall. It's a great place to get a good deal on turquoise jewelry.

Dream Catcher Inn
10201 Starfly Road
Las Cruces, NM 88011
(505) 522-3035
www.dreamcatcherinn.com

Inn of the Anasazi

SANTA FE, NEW MEXICO

*L*ocation is very important in Santa Fe, especially for travelers who want to explore the downtown plaza area. The streets are narrow, parking is at a premium, and it's just easier to walk than it is to drive in this historic section of town. The good news is, the accessible Inn of the Anasazi is conveniently located just steps from the downtown plaza. This 57-room property includes one accessible guest room (Room 103) and makes an excellent home base for Santa Fe sightseers.

Named for the group of Native Americans who inhabited the area and then mysteriously disappeared some 700 years ago, the property includes a number of uniquely Southwestern architectural features such as hand-carved entry doors, traditional viga ceilings, sandstone walls, and kiva fireplaces. But the architecture is just part of the inn's charm, as this property is also well known for its high level of personal service.

General manager Jeff Mahan puts a strong emphasis on customer service; he realizes that satisfied customers will return time after time. This attitude is reflected in the actions of employees like Lisa Hendrix. As Lisa was showing me the amenities of my room she reminded me about the dry air and pointed out the humidifier in the room. "If you are not used to the dry air, it can disrupt your sleep patterns," said Lisa. "Turning on the humidifier will help you have a more restful night." Indeed, it's those personal touches that really make a difference.

And those personal touches start at the front door, where valet parking is the standard operating procedure. "Because of the lack of parking spaces near the inn, valet parking is just more convenient for all of our guests," says Lisa, "but of course people who can't walk long distances especially appreciate this service."

The inn features level access to the spacious lobby, through wide double doors. Room 103 is located on the first floor, near the end of a wide hallway. Access features include wide doorways, lever handles, good pathway access, and lowered closet rods. A large four-poster bed is the centerpiece of

The bathroom in Room 103 at the Inn of the Anasazi features a tub/shower combination and fold–down grab bars by the toilet.

the room, and although it's 28" high, it was chosen because it's considerably lower than standard beds of the same design. A gas fireplace tops off the creature comforts of the room.

The bathroom has a tub/shower combination with a hand-held showerhead. A portable shower bench is available upon request. There are grab bars in the shower and fold-down grab bars on one side of the toilet. A small side table partially blocks access to the roll-under sink, but Liz is quick to point out that it is removed when the room is occupied by a wheelchair-user. All in all it's a very comfortable room.

There is barrier-free access to all the first-floor public areas including the library, the living room, and the Anasazi Restaurant.

The nightly rate for Room 103 ranges from $199 to $299.

The inn is located just a few blocks from the Palace of the Governors, the Museum of Fine Arts, and the Georgia O'Keefe Museum, all of which are wheelchair-accessible. Santa Fe is a great city to explore on foot, as the downtown area sidewalks have curb-cuts, and most of the shops and restaurants have level access. Additionally, the lift-equipped M Line bus runs from the Sheridan Street station to Museum Hill, where four more museums are located.

Indeed, you can spend a whole week just enjoying the museums and cultural attractions in the area. And the Inn of the Anasazi is the perfect place to rest your head each night.

Inn of the Anasazi
113 Washington Avenue
Santa Fe, NM 87501
(505) 988-3030
www.innoftheanasazi.com

The San Geronimo Lodge

TAOS, NEW MEXICO

*P*at Hoffman is not a newcomer to innkeeping or to barrier-free design. In fact, by the time she purchased the San Geronimo Lodge in Taos, she had already added an accessible unit to her previous B&B in Key West, Florida.

Says Pat about her decision to add barrier-free features to her first inn, "I was inspired by a wedding guest, the father of a groom, who stayed in one of our regular kitchen units. He needed assistance to enter the building, which had one small step. I knew right then I needed to do something to make my inn accessible to all guests."

Since the San Geronimo Lodge was in need of some major repairs when Pat purchased it in 1994, it seemed only natural for her to include access upgrades in the renovations. Pat recounts, "Twelve of the 18 units had been destroyed by a previous tenant. In our discussions with the architect about the renovation, we stipulated that two of the units should be accessible. We had previously worked with Susan Behart in Florida and requested her help in configuring these two units."

Today this 18-room B&B includes two wheelchair-accessible guest rooms, Room 4 and Room 5. The main entrance to the lodge has one small step, but the accessible entrance is located near Rooms 4 and 5 on the south side of the East Wing. Accessible parking is located on the east side of the building, with a paved pathway to the accessible entrance.

Access features in Room 4 and Room 5 include wide doorways, level thresholds, open-frame beds, and good pathway access. Room 4 has one queen-sized bed and Room 5 has two twin beds. Each of the bathrooms has a roll-in shower with a hand-held showerhead, a shower bench, grab bars in the shower and around the toilet, a tilted mirror, a roll-under sink, and a raised toilet. Both accessible guest rooms also have a kiva fireplace.

The public breakfast area has good access, with an extra wide doorway and plenty of room between the tables. Wheelchair-accessible restrooms are located near the dining room. The pitch of the ramp between the gift shop and the lobby is slightly steeper than code, but it's doable for most wheelchair-users. There is also a level aggregate garden walkway just outside of the accessible rooms. All in all, Pat did a great job adding accessible features to this historic adobe lodge.

The nightly rate for Room 4 or Room 5 is $115.

The San Geronimo Lodge is located just five minutes from the Taos Plaza, which features a number of galleries and shops. Says Pat, "Most of the galleries and museums (except the Fechin which is in an historic home) in Taos are accessible. I believe most of the classes of the Taos Institute of Art are also accessible."

The Taos Pueblo is one of the biggest attractions in the area, and it's generally accessible to wheelchair-users in dry weather. There are level dirt pathways through the pueblo, but some of the buildings have narrow doorways or steps. Outdoor recreation is a big draw during the winter months. "Taos Ski Valley has provisions for people with mobility disabilities," says Pat. "One of our staff people who works on the mountain in the winter says the lifts can accommodate wheelchair-users and that there are special instructors on the staff."

The bottom line is that the San Geronimo Lodge delights in serving a diverse group of guests, with the emphasis on service. Says Pat, "We want all of our guests to enjoy their stay with us."

The San Geronimo Lodge
1101 Witt Road
Taos, NM 87571
(505) 751-3776
www.sangeronimolodge.com

The Inn at Cooperstown

COOPERSTOWN, NEW YORK

*B*uilt as a hotel in 1874, The Inn at Cooperstown was fully restored in 1984 by the previous innkeeper, Michael Jerome. Says Michael about the access improvements, "Long before the ADA was in effect, we were committed to making the property accessible to many different travelers. In addition to adding a wheelchair-accessible room to the inventory, we also incorporated suggestions from our disabled guests over the years. To that end we added features like hanging racks at two heights and a portable bathroom stool to the accessible guest room. We learned something from each guest, since every traveler has their own needs."

Today innkeepers Marc and Sherrie Kingsley carry on Michael's vision as they continue to welcome all guests to their inn. Located in the heart of Cooperstown, this historic inn features 17 guest rooms, including one (Room 11) that is wheelchair-accessible.

With ramp access from the parking area nearby, this first-floor room features wide doorways, a pocket door to the bathroom, and good pathway access throughout the room. The bathroom has a low-step shower with a shower seat, a hand-held showerhead, grab bars in the shower, and a roll-under sink. Although there is lip on the shower it is still possible to transfer to the shower seat from a wheelchair.

All of the first-floor public rooms, including two sitting rooms, two dining rooms, and a meeting room, feature barrier-free access. Outside, the perennial garden is also accessible to wheelchair-users. There is one step down to the spacious verandah, but there is an accessible seating area adjacent to the porch.

Rates for Room 11 range from $99 to $187 per night. The lowest rates are available on weekdays from January to March.

The biggest attraction in the area is the National Baseball Hall of Fame, which is located just a short walk from the inn. Other accessible attractions in the area include the Fenimore Art Museum and the Farmers' Museum. Because of the central location of the Inn at Cooperstown, it's the ideal lodging choice for people who want to explore the local sights.

The Inn at Cooperstown
16 Chestnut Street
Cooperstown, NY 13326
(607) 547-5756
www.innatcooperstown.com

The Jefferson Inn

ELLICOTTVILLE, NEW YORK

*F*rom the moment she first spotted the elegant village home that would someday become the Jefferson Inn, Donna Gushue just knew it had be a B&B. So she stepped up to the plate, so to speak, and purchased the property. After a few renovations she welcomed her first guests and entered a new profession. Today Donna is an old hand at innkeeping, and her five-room Jefferson Inn attracts guests who want to relax and enjoy the small-town ambiance of Ellicottville, an undiscovered jewel in Western New York.

In hindsight, Donna makes no bones about why she made her property accessible. "I was not required to put in an accessible room," she says. "I just believe in making rooms accessible because I used to work as a public health nurse and I know how difficult it is for disabled travelers."

So when the inn was renovated in 1994, she unofficially added a downstairs accessible room. Although this room is not listed in the on-line inventory, guests can book it by calling the inn directly. Says Donna, "The accessible room is not in our on-line availability calendar because we must take another room out of service if we book it. We also want to make sure that we have the degree of accessibility needed, so we prefer to talk to guests before they book the room."

The accessible guest room (which doesn't have a name) is located on the first floor and features ramp access through the side room. "I had a person in a power wheelchair see if he could get up the ramp, through the door and into the room, as well as out the other door onto our beautiful wrap-around porch," recalls Donna. "He had no problems accessing anything."

Access features in the accessible bathroom include a low-step shower with a fold-down shower seat and a hand-held showerhead, a raised toilet with grab bars, and a roll-under sink. "I had an occupational therapist give me advice before renovating," adds Donna.

The first-floor public areas, including the living room, porch and dining room, all have good pathway access and adequate room for a wheelchair to maneuver. Donna notes one seasonal problem with access to the inn. "Our inn is sometimes not accessible via the ramp during the winter season," she explains. "If there is an ice hazard on the roof we have to close the ramp until the ice falls. If someone can walk up three steps then they can get into the house in winter."

The nightly rates for the accessible room range from $89 to $159. Winter is the peak season at the Jefferson Inn as it is located in a ski resort area.

The Inn is just a half block away from Main Street. Says Donna, "There are a dozen restaurants and many gift shops on Main Street, many of which are accessible from the sidewalk. During the warmer months you can sit at outside tables and watch the world go by."

During the winter, thoughts turn to skiing. "Both our ski hills have special programs for people with disabilities," says Donna. "One of my acquaintances is a recent double amputee, and she has had excellent help here in learning to ski. I can link guests up with either of the adaptive ski programs."

The Jefferson Inn
3 Jefferson Street
Ellicottville, NY 14731
(716) 699-5869
www.thejeffersoninn.com

Hawkesdene House

ANDREWS, NORTH CAROLINA

*N*estled in a private cove adjoining the Nantahala National Forest, Hawkesdene House offers guests the charm and comfort of an English country house combined with the rustic beauty of the North Carolina mountains. The inn has five B&B rooms and four private cottages, including one first-floor guest room and a wheelchair-accessible cottage.

Owners Roy and Daphne Sargent opened the inn in 1995, and because of his own personal experiences Roy has a good understanding of access issues. "I had the same injury that Christopher Reeves had," says Roy. "Although I have recovered to the extent that I do not need a wheelchair, I was faced with that possibility and am very aware of the difficulties. So, when we built our cottages in 1997, I made sure one of them (the Primrose Cottage) was wheelchair-accessible."

The two-bedroom Primrose Cottage has a queen-sized bed in one bedroom, two twin beds in the other bedroom, and a sleeper sofa in the living room. There is ramped access to the front door and wide doorways and good pathway access throughout the cottage. The bathroom has a tub/shower combination, a hand-held shower, and grab bars in the tub area and around the raised toilet. A portable shower chair is available upon request. Outside, there is level access to the private barbecue area.

Over at the main house, the Snowbird Room is a good choice for guests who cannot manage stairs, but who do not need full wheelchair access. There is level access to the inn from the deck. The Snowbird Room features a queen-sized bed, a private bathroom, and a beautiful view of the Snowbird Mountains. Access features include wide doorways, grab bars around the raised toilet, and glass shower doors that can be removed upon request.

The first-floor public areas of the inn are also nicely accessible The great room, dining rooms, and outside deck all feature level access and wide doorways. The outside deck is level with the adjacent parking area and the main floor of the inn.

Nightly rates for the Primrose Cottage range from $359 to $429. The Snowbird Room rents for $119 per night.

Roy is full of suggestions for accessible activities in the area. "The Nantahala National Forest recently opened a wheelchair hiking trail," says Roy. "It's paved and it has a special bridge across the Nantahala River. It's about three miles long and it's beautiful. The trailhead is about 10 miles from our inn."

Roy also recommends gem mining. "It's a good activity for wheelchair-users," he explains. "They bring you a bucket of mud and you look for gems by washing the mud in a screen. A trough of water runs through the center of your picnic table. The gem-mining place is about 20 miles away and it's great fun."

Of course, one of the best things to do at Hawkesdene House is to just relax and enjoy the scenery. As Roy puts it, "We have a little piece of heaven, right here in North Carolina!"

Hawkesdene House
381 Phillips Creek Road
Andrews, NC 28901
(828) 321-6027
www.hawkesdene.com

Theodosia's B&B

*L*ocated on Bald Head Island just two miles off the North Carolina coast, Theodosia's B&B offers guests the ambiance of yesteryear and the accessibility of today. This Victorian-style B&B was constructed in 1995, and it features 14 upscale guest rooms, including the accessible Heidi Rose room.

Former owner Garrett Albertson points out the popularity of the Heidi Rose room. "We welcomed a number of wheelchair-users who really enjoyed that room," he recalls. "In fact, for two years we hosted patients from the Cheny Clinic, so we paid particular attention to the physical access of the inn."

The first-floor Heidi Rose room has wide doorways, good pathway access and a queen-sized sleigh bed. Access features include a roll-in shower with a fold-down shower seat and level access to the wraparound porch through a set of wide French doors. There is ramp access to the porch from the nearby parking lot, so guests can access the Heidi Rose room either from the porch or from the interior of the inn. The dining room, living room, and wraparound porch are all on the same level. The Heidi Rose room also features great views of the Old Baldy lighthouse and Bald Head Creek.

As an added bonus all inn guests are provided with an electric cart for their transportation on the island. Says Garrett, "The cart for the Heidi Rose room is parked at the bottom of the ramp, and it is a simple process to strap a wheelchair on the back of the cart."

Rates for the Heidi Rose room range from $155 to $225 per night. The lowest rates are available from November to March.

Bald Head Island is only accessible by ferry or private boat. The ferry is ramped, and wheelchair-users can ride on the open deck in good weather. In inclement weather the crew will assist them over the raised threshold into the protected passenger compartment.

Garrett is full of accessible sightseeing suggestions. "Sandpiper Beach has been constructed for accessibility, and a beach wheelchair is available for loan at the fire department," he says. Indeed the chief attraction of Bald

Head Island is its unspoiled natural beauty. "Disabled guests have expressed appreciation for the ease in which they may explore the natural beauty of this place," adds Garrett. "Guests just love to explore the island in the electric golf carts."

Theodosia's B&B
Harbour Village
Bald Head Island, NC 28461
(910) 457-6563
www.theodosias.com

Sunset Inn

*T*he Sunset Inn is located on the island of Sunset Beach, approximately 30 minutes north of Myrtle Beach and 40 minutes south of Wilmington. This 14-room inn was constructed in 2000, and as innkeeper Andrea Suggs notes, "Local building codes mandated the inclusion of accessible features."

"Under the law we had to make at least one of our guest rooms wheelchair-accessible," says Andrea. "But I think we would have done that anyway, even if there wasn't any law, because it's very hard to find a place to rent that is wheelchair-accessible."

Built on pilings, the Sunset Inn features elevator access from the ground level up to the first floor. The accessible Live Oak Suite is located near the elevator on the first floor. It has a king-sized bed, a love seat, an entertainment center, a small refrigerator, a wet bar, and a private screened porch that overlooks the Intracoastal Waterway. Access features include wide doorways and good pathway access, and the spacious bathroom has a roll-in shower with a hand-held showerhead and a fold-down shower seat, a roll-under sink, and a five-foot turning radius.

Rates for the Live Oak Suite range from $85 to $150 per night. The rates are highest in peak season, during the summer months.

After they unpack, most of Andrea's guests head to the beach. Says Andrea, "Ocean Isle Beach is the next beach over, about seven miles. They also have beach wheelchairs at no charge."

"I suppose the big attraction to Sunset Beach is that we are a nice quiet family beach," says Andrea. "We are connected to the mainland by a bridge and we are within driving distance of Myrtle Beach and Wilmington. Our location makes us very convenient to all types of entertainment, but our guests come back here to enjoy the quiet comfort of the inn and Sunset Beach."

Sunset Inn
9 North Shore Drive
Sunset Beach, N.C. 28468
(910) 575-1000
www.thesunsetinn.net

Mast Farm Inn

VALLE CRUCIS, NORTH CAROLINA

T he Mast Farm Inn is a full-service country inn located in the historic community of Valle Crucis in the mountains of North Carolina. Placed on the National Register of Historic Places in 1972, the inn is a good example of an early American farmstead. The three-story farmhouse has eight guest rooms and four detached cottages.

Says innkeeper Wanda Hinshaw, "The inn was restored in 1985 by the previous owners. They had the foresight to make the public restrooms and one guest room in the farmhouse accessible. When it became necessary for us to convert the accessible guest room to the dining room, we felt we needed to provide an accessible accommodation to replace it. So, when we built the two new cottages in 2000, we designed the Gazebo Cottage to meet this need."

Cottage parking is available in a nearby gravel lot. A flagstone terrace leads from the parking area to the wooden access ramp for the Gazebo Cottage. The 600-square-foot cottage has an open floor plan and plenty of room to wheel around. Although the high king-sized bed may present a difficult transfer for some wheelchair-users, a single trundle bed is stored underneath. The large bathroom has a roll-in shower and a roll-under sink. There is also level access to the open porch, which runs the entire length of the cottage.

Some guests will need to drive to the main farmhouse from the Gazebo Cottage, as the lighted path through the pine woods is not wheelchair-accessible. The yard that leads to it is quite steep as well.

Over at the farmhouse, there is ramp access to the porch and level access to the first-floor dining room, public restrooms, parlor and gift shop. Says Wanda, "We rebuilt the ramp to the porch several years ago to replace one that was quite steep. A gentleman in a wheelchair who used to visit our restaurant prompted us to do it."

The nightly rates for the Gazebo Cottage range from $275 to $285.

As far as sightseeing goes, Wanda's top pick is the spectacular scenery on the Blue Ridge Parkway. "I believe there is an elevator at Grandfather Mountain, making the view and the mile-high bridge accessible," she advises. "I have also seen wheelchairs at Price Lake, in one of the federal parks along the parkway. And our own Valle Crucis Community Park has a mile-long paved trail."

Besides the historic feel of the Mast Farm Inn, it also has a very relaxed and comfortable atmosphere. "We pride ourselves in our sincere hospitality," adds Wanda.

Mast Farm Inn
2543 Broadstone Road
Valle Crucis, NC 28691
(828) 963-5857
www.mastfarminn.com

HideAway
Country Inn

BUCYRUS, OHIO

*B*ordered by cornfields, the HideAway Country Inn is surrounded by 400 acres of farmland just outside of Bucyrus, Ohio. It is a true country inn in every sense of the definition. Even the driving directions remind guests to look for the "six shiny grain bins" that mark the turn into the inn's driveway, because after all, "landmarks are important when you are in the middle of a corn field."

But don't expect a rickety one-room inn with shared bathroom facilities at this country inn. Billed as a luxury inn, this rural property is also a popular wedding venue and a great choice for romantic weekend retreats. And as innkeeper Debbie Miller points out, "Nature lovers also enjoy our property because of the 22 acres of wooded hiking paths along our northern border."

A combination of events—including aging parents and grandparents—led to Debbie's decision to add the accessible Louis XIV Suite to her inventory. "We had a number of guests who requested rooms without stairs, and one thing led to another, so when we added our suites we decided to make one of them wheelchair-accessible. After all, everybody should be able to enjoy our inn."

The Louis XIV Suite is located in HideAway Hall, which is detached from the main building. Accessible parking is available in a paved lot, located halfway between the main building and HideAway Hall. The Louis XIV Suite has a hallway entrance and a back patio entrance, both of which feature wide doorways and level thresholds.

The Louis XIV Suite takes its name from a massive Louis XIV-style canopy bed purchased from the Plaza Hotel in New York City. Debbie is quick to point out that the bed is functional as well as attractive. "This bed is unique as the height is adjustable," she says. "You can raise or lower it for an easier

The Louis XIV Suite is located in HideAway Hall,
the newest building at HideAway Country Inn.

transfer. Sometimes these kinds of beds are way too high for wheelchair-users." The romantic ambiance of the suite is further enhanced by a three-sided glass fireplace and a (non-accessible) Jacuzzi tub in the bedroom area.

Access features include wide doorways and good pathway access throughout the suite. The bathroom has a roll-in shower with a fold-down shower seat, a hand-held showerhead, grab bars in the shower and around the toilet, and a roll-under sink. Breakfast is served in the dining room in the main house, or (with advance arrangements) it can be delivered to your room.

There is ramped access to the main house, where the dining room and meeting room are located. Two outdoor patios are also available for dining. The inn restaurant is open to the public for dinner, but reservations are recommended.

Nightly room rates for the Louis XIV Suite range from $177 to $257. A number of romantic packages and add-ons are also available.

According to Debbie, "Farm land and the farm experience is the big attraction in the area. Many of our guests like to visit Cooper's Mill in Bucyrus to watch them make their jams and jellies." The Cooper's Mill tour is available during the week, but I have to admit a very accommodating employee showed me the factory on the weekend. There is level access to the factory, but the accessible entry to the store (through the back door) is a bit hard to find. Still, it's worth a stop.

Nature lovers should head over to Lowe-Volk park, where they will find an accessible nature center and bird viewing station. There is also an unpaved level trail over a grassy area next door to the nature center. It's doable by most in dry weather, but after a rain the mud makes it very difficult to navigate in a wheelchair. It's a prime place for birders in the spring!

HideAway Country Inn
1601 State Route 4
Bucyrus, OH 44820
(419) 562-3013
www.hideawayinn.com

Hocking Hills Retreat

LOGAN, OHIO

*L*ocated just an hour from Columbus in Southeast Ohio, the Hocking Hills area is noted for its natural beauty. Indeed, it's an ideal off-the-beaten-path getaway destination. Fortunately "off-the-beaten-path" (in this case) doesn't translate into "wheelers not welcome," as innkeeper Ellen Grinsfelder has gone out of her way to make her Inn at Cedar Falls very accessible.

The Inn at Cedar Falls, which is adjacent to Hocking Hills State Park, features B&B rooms, detached cottages, and log cabins. Accessible lodging options include the Redbud Cabin and the Sumac Cottage.

Says Ellen, "Many years ago a guest told me that although a lot of inns claim to be accessible, very few actually get it right. When we built Redbud, I wanted to make sure it was truly accessible, so I hired a local access consultant." Ellen's efforts definitely paid off.

The Redbud Cabin at the Inn at Cedar Falls
features ramped access to the front door.

The nicely accessible Redbud Cabin features ramped access to the front door, wide doorways, and good pathway access to the first-floor kitchen, bedroom, bathroom, living area, and back porch. The first-floor bathroom features a roll-in shower with a hand-held showerhead, grab bars in the shower and around the toilet, a roll-under sink, and a portable shower bench. The second-floor bedroom and bathroom are only accessible by a flight of stairs, but it's a great option for kids, attendants, or able-bodied friends.

The cottages are a more recent addition to the inn. When they were constructed in 2003, Ellen responded to a guest's request to make at least one wheelchair-accessible. Less than a year later, the Sumac Cottage was opened.

The Sumac Cottage features ramped access to front door from the driveway, wide doorways, and good pathway access throughout the spacious living and bedroom area. The bathroom has a roll-in shower with a hand-held showerhead, grab bars in the shower and around the toilet, a roll-under sink, and a lowered mirror. Other cabin features include an under-counter refrigerator, a spacious back porch, and a (non-accessible) whirlpool tub in the living area. A portable shower bench is available upon request.

There is also level access to most of the inn's public areas, including the office, gift shop, bar, and outside breakfast area. Guests will need to drive down to the main office area for breakfast, but accessible parking is available right next to the accessible entrance to the restaurant.

Nightly rates for the Redbud Cabin range from $159 to $229. Rates for the Sumac Cottage range from $139 to $209 per night. The lowest rates are available on weekdays from December to March (excluding holiday periods).

As for local attractions, Ellen is quick to point out that Mother Nature is the number-one tourist draw in the area. Says Ellen, "People come here to enjoy the natural beauty of the waterfalls, rock formations and caves. Gladly there are also a few accessible choices. Wheelchair-users can explore accessible trails at nearby Ash Cave and Conkle's Hollow, and of course the whole area makes a beautiful fall foliage driving tour."

All in all, the Inn at Cedar Falls is a very accessible place to relax and enjoy the surrounding beauty. As one former guest puts it, "The wheelchair access at this inn is a rare and appreciated plus."

Inn at Cedar Falls
21190 State Route 374
Logan, OH 43138
(740) 385-7489
www.innatcedarfalls.com

The Inn at Honey Run

MILLERSBURG, OHIO

I first learned about the Inn at Honey Run from an *Emerging Horizons* subscriber who wrote, "It is one of the most accessible places I have ever stayed." Several years later I had the chance to experience the inn myself, and I'm pleased to report that the original description was not an exaggeration. Not only is the Inn at Honey Run very accessible, it also has perhaps the most accommodating staff I have ever encountered. These folks know good service, they know how to make people feel comfortable, and (best of all) they really (really) love their jobs. Indeed, it's a tough combination to beat.

Named for the gentle brook (Honey Run) found on the property, the Inn at Honey Run is located in the heart of Ohio Amish Country, halfway between Berlin and Millersburg. That said, it's not your typical Amish country inn. In fact the architecture is reminiscent of Frank Lloyd Wright's work; contemporary lines blended into a natural setting. The main lodge features 25 guest rooms, including Room 121, which is wheelchair-accessible.

Access was built into the inn from the beginning, under the watchful eye of former owner Marge Stock. Marge went above and beyond the minimum access standards. Says innkeeper Phil Jenkins, "Marge wanted to make sure the inn was really accessible. For example, she made sure that the accessible room had a true roll-in shower—not one of those that is too small or has a lip. She even installed a roll-in shower in her own home." Marge sold the property to Phil in January 2003, and thankfully Phil carries on Marge's customer-service attitude—he makes sure everybody fully enjoys their stay.

Accessible parking is available near the main entrance, which is actually located on the second floor of the inn. Most of the public rooms are also located on the second floor, but there is elevator access to all three floors. Room 121 is located on the first floor.

Room 121 features a nice view of the surrounding woods. Access features include wide doorways and excellent pathway access throughout the guest room. The bathroom has a large roll-in shower with a hand-held show-

Room 121 at The Inn at Honey Run features
wide doorway access to the bathroom.

erhead and grab bars in the shower and around the toilet. Two shower seat options (a chair and a bench) are available. The sink is located in the guest room area, right outside the bathroom.

There is level access to all public areas, including the lobby, game room, gift shop, and dining room. A complimentary continental breakfast is served to inn guests every morning. In the afternoons and evenings the dining room is open to the public and features American regional cuisine. Dinner entrees range from sesame-encrusted walleye to pan seared duck breast with sun-dried apricot-cranberry chutney . During the summer months an outdoor cafe also serves sandwiches at lunch.

A number of nature trails dot the 60-acre estate; the most accessible one being a half-mile loop along the river. This dirt trail is covered with wood chips, and although it's fairly level the trailhead is quite a downhill hike from the main building. It's not a big problem though, as Phil assures me that gator and golf cart transportation is available for people who cannot make it to the trailhead. "Or," Phil adds, "you can just ask us to take you along the whole trail in the gator or golf cart. It's a beautiful area and nobody should miss out on it."

Nightly rates for Room 121 range from $99 to $154. The lowest rates are available on weekdays from January through March.

Amish culture is the big draw in the area, and there are many accessible Amish attractions. The Behalt Mennonite Information Center offers a good overview of Amish and Mennonite history, while Yoder's Amish Home gives visitors a glimpse of daily Amish life. Don't miss the Holmes Country Amish Flea Market (Thursday through Saturday); a great place to shop for Amish crafts, clothing, and homemade goodies. And of course the whole county makes a great road-trip destination. It's especially scenic during the fall foliage season.

The Inn at Honey Run
6920 County Road 203
Millersburg, OH 44654
(330) 674-0011
www.innathoneyrun.com

Shiloh Morning Inn

ARDMORE, OKLAHOMA

B ob and Linda Humphrey welcomed their first guests to the Shiloh Morning Inn on July 1, 1999. "Since we built our facility from scratch, it was a simple matter to add an accessible room," says Linda. "We felt it was a part of the service we wanted to offer our guests." Ironically, Linda was the first person to test out their new accessible facilities. "Since I fell during our move and was in a wheelchair for six weeks, we both came to appreciate the need for an accessible lodging facility," Linda recalls.

The Shiloh Morning Inn has five suites in the main house and four detached cottages. Accessible parking is located close to the front of the main house, with sidewalk access to the ramped front porch. The front entrance has a wide doorway and level threshold access to the inn.

Suite Memories, the accessible guest room, features a king-sized bed, a corner fireplace, and a sitting area with tables and chairs. There is good pathway access throughout this spacious first-floor suite.

Of course construction of the accessible guest room didn't exactly go off without a hitch. Originally the roll-in shower was installed with a one-inch lip, so Linda had a metal worker fashion a removable threshold ramp to remedy the problem. Other bathroom access features include a built-in shower seat and grab bars in the shower and around the toilet. There is also a separate (non-accessible) soaking tub in the bathroom.

Breakfast is served in the tiled dining room, located on the first floor. The parlor and library feature low-pile carpet for easy wheeling. Since the inn is located on rolling hills, most of the outdoor areas around the property are not wheelchair-accessible. On the other hand, Donna says, "Many of our slow walker guests enjoy the nearby walking trails dotted with park benches and hammocks."

The nightly rate for Suite Memories is $175.

Admittedly, the main attraction in the area is the great outdoors. Linda is happy to give guests driving directions for a day drive out to one of the parks.

"Most of our guests come here for the peace and quiet," says Linda. "Since dinner is available and a three-course breakfast is included, most of our guests find us a destination resort. We are a short 20-minute drive from I35 and only two hours from Dallas or Oklahoma City."

Apparently Linda and Bob are doing something right, as they seem to have a steady stream of repeat customers. Adds Linda, "Our disabled guests who come again and again tell us we have given them a new choice for their getaways."

Shiloh Morning Inn
2179 Ponderosa Road
Ardmore, OK 73401
(580) 223-9500
www.ShilohMorning.com

St. Bernard's B&B

*L*ocated on the rugged Oregon coast, St. Bernard's B&B is a storybook chateau filled with French antiques. At first glance it looks like a castle. This 10,000-square-foot property was constructed in 1995 as the dream home of Don Bernard, and because of his previous experience with a temporary disability, Don took special care to incorporate access features into the design.

Says Don, "My wife had a skiing accident and was in a wheelchair for almost two years. I became frustrated and angry at the inconveniences we had to endure, and swore that if I could, I would try to make a difference." And it appears he has made that difference.

There is ramp access to the tiled reception area, and the accessible Parisian Room is located on the first floor. The Parisian Room features hand-painted European wallpaper, a carved armoire, and a queen-sized bed. The bathroom sink has a removable pedestal base that allows for roll-under access. There are grab bars around the toilet, and the low step shower (five-inch lip) has a hand-held showerhead and a shower bench.

There is level access to the first-floor public areas, including the patio, front deck, living room (where wine is served in the evening), and conservatory (where breakfast is served).

The rate for the Parisian Room is $149 per night.

One of the big attractions in the area is the scenic Oregon Coast, and St. Bernard's is located just 250 yards from a beautiful white sand beach. If you'd like to go into town, Don suggests Cannon Beach, which is about four miles away. "Cannon Beach is pretty friendly to wheelchairs as a result of a lawsuit by a local with multiple sclerosis," says Don. "The town is reminiscent of Carmel, California, about thirty years ago. There are lots of galleries and no T-shirt shops, fast food joints, or neon signs. It's just a nice little town."

St. Bernard's B&B
3 E. Ocean Road
Arch Cape, OR 97102
(503) 436-2800
www.st-bernards.com

Beach House B&B

*I*f I only had two words to describe the Beach House B&B, they would be "casual luxury." Located in the heart of Nye Beach, this two-room inn is an excellent choice for a relaxing, romantic getaway. Innkeeper Pat McGuire caters to her guests, yet she's not overbearing. Indeed, privacy is the keyword here.

The Coast Street Room is a good choice for slow walkers and some wheelchair-users, as you can park on the street, near the front door. This ground-floor suite includes a king-sized bed, a gas fireplace, a refrigerator, and a microwave. There is level access to the suite and plenty of room to maneuver; however, the bathroom is not adapted.

The bathroom has a pedestal sink and a standard shower and toilet. It's best suited for somebody who can walk at least a few steps, as there aren't

The Coast Street Room at the Beach House B&B
features a king-sized bed in the spacious suite.

any grab bars and there isn't room for a direct transfer to the toilet. Still, it's a huge suite and it will work for many people.

Breakfast is delivered via the dumbwaiter, so you can enjoy it at your leisure in the privacy of your own room.

The rate for the Coast Room is $110 per night.

For dinner, Pat suggests ARR Place, which is wheelchair-accessible and located just around the corner. The Nye Beach area is a typical funky beach town with shops and restaurants and tons of ambiance. Parking is located near 3rd Street and Coast Drive, and there is a ramp down to the sandy beach area. Some of the old shops are not accessible, but it's a nice place to just sit and watch the ocean. Nearby accessible sightseeing options include the Oregon Coast Aquarium and the Yaquina Head Lighthouse (the inside is not accessible, but there is a great boardwalk viewing area behind the lighthouse).

And don't miss the wheelchair-accessible tidepools at Yaquina Head. Yes, that's right, I said wheelchair-accessible tidepools. Wheelchair-users can park in the lower parking lot at Quarry Cove, and just roll down to the tidepools. The paved paths go right into the intertidal area. There are also raised tidepools, which are just the right viewing height for wheelers. It's all very accessible and it's great place to get a up-close-and-personal with the local marine life.

Beach House B&B
107 SW Coast Street
Newport OR 97365
(541) 265-9141
www.beachhousebb.com

Seaside Inn

SEASIDE, OREGON

*B*illed as the ultimate oceanfront bed and breakfast hotel, the Seaside Inn is located directly on the Promenade in the quaint coastal town of Seaside, Oregon. Says innkeeper Susan Peters, "We're small enough to give guests friendly, personalized attention, yet large enough to offer much more than typical bed and breakfast establishments." These added extras include chef-prepared "anytime" meals, a full service bar, a library, VCRs, and a massage therapist.

Attention is also paid to access at the Seaside Inn. Changing times and an aging family member motivated Susan to include an accessible guest room in her 14-room inn. The accessible Shell Seeker Room is located on the second floor, and it features beautiful ocean views and a cozy gas fireplace.

Access features in the Shell Seeker Room include wide doorways and good pathway access. The bathroom has a roll-in shower with grab bars and a hand-held showerhead. A portable shower chair is available upon request.

There are wide doorways throughout the public areas of the inn and elevator access to all floors. Breakfast is served in the first-floor oceanfront gathering room.

Rates for the Shell Seeker room range from $115 to $195 per night. The rates are dependent on the day of the week and the length of the stay.

As for accessible diversions in Seaside, Susan says, "Seaside is a very wheelchair-friendly town. In 2000, the city constructed a large cement ramp that goes right down to the beach." She adds, "Our property sits right on a two-mile sidewalk that runs parallel to the beach."

Seaside Inn
581 South Promenade
Seaside, OR 97138
(503) 738-6403
www.theseasideinn.com

Blue Ball B&B

Located in the heart of Pennsylvania Amish Country, the Blue Ball B&B is the perfect place to unwind and take a step back in time. According to innkeeper Jeanne Warsheski, "It's not uncommon for guests to hear the clip-clopping of Amish buggies as they are escorted to their rooms."

The accessible Cherry Room was added to this six-room inn during a remodeling project. "There seemed to be a demand for it," says Jeanne. "So when we put the bathroom in the Cherry Room we decided to make it accessible." But the bathroom isn't the only thing accessible about this property. Accessible parking is located approximately 30 feet from the house, and there is ramp access to the inn from the driveway. A level threshold at the entrance makes the entire first floor wheelchair-accessible. The Cherry Room features a queen-sized bed, a wood-burning fireplace, wide doorways, and good pathway access. Says Jean, "The entire first floor (including the Cherry Room) has hardwood floors. At least five guests have told us this feature makes it easier to maneuver in a wheelchair."

This spacious 16' x 20' Cherry Room features sliding-door access to the bathroom. Access features in the bathroom include a roll-in shower with a hand-held showerhead and a built-in shower bench, grab bars in the shower and around the toilet, a raised toilet, and a roll-under sink.

The rate for the Cherry Room is $80 per night, but if you stay for a week you only have to pay for four nights. The Blue Ball B&B is located just 45 minutes from Hershey and 1 hour 15 minutes from Gettysburg and Philadelphia, so there are many day-trip possibilities. Suggests Jeanne, "We are close to the Millenium Theatre, which puts on a live biblical story production. There is also lots of shopping here; including outlets, Amish stores and several farmers' markets. Hershey Park is another popular guest choice."

Blue Ball B&B
1075 Main Street
Blue Ball, PA 17506
(717) 355-9994
www.blueballbandb.com

Fairville Inn

Surrounded by majestic homes and miles of back roads, the 15-room Fairville Inn is located in the scenic Brandywine Valley. Although the main house was built in 1857 and is listed on the National Register of Historic Places, former owners Tom and Eleanor Everitt made it as accessible as possible. Tom is quick to point out, however, that "the property isn't totally wheelchair-accessible, but it's still a good choice for many slow walkers or part time wheelchair-users." Today Jane and Noel McStay operate the inn.

There is a ramped entrance to the main house from the nearby parking lot and plenty of room to park in the oversized parking lot, which serves the three buildings of the inn. The accessible room (named Main House 1) is located on the first floor of the main house.

Main House 1 has a queen-sized bed and plenty of room to maneuver in a wheelchair. The bathroom has a tub/shower combination and a bench seat in the tub. The space below the sink is closed, and it does not allow roll-under access. There are no grab bars on the walls around the toilet, but a raised toilet seat with attached grab bars can be added upon request.

The breakfast area is also located on the first floor. Outside, the access is weather dependent. The three acres of open space that surround the inn are generally wheelchair-accessible in the dry season.

The rate for Main House 1 is $150 per night.

The Fairville Inn is located just 13 miles from Wilmington, Delaware; where the accessible Christina Waterfront is a big draw. Flanked by an urban wildlife refuge on one end and a riverfront park on the other, this revitalized waterfront area features a bevy of shops, restaurants, and entertainment venues, connected by a 1.3-mile accessible riverfront walkway.

To be honest, one of the main attractions of this area is the natural beauty. Indeed, there are a lot of scenic drives throughout the Brandywine Valley.

Fairville Inn
506 Kennett Pike
Chadds Ford, PA 19317
(610) 388-5900
www.fairvilleinn.com

Two Suns Inn

BEAUFORT, SOUTH CAROLINA

The Two Suns Inn features upscale accommodations on the scenic South Carolina coast. Housed in a historic home, this six-room inn is located on the bay, midway between Charleston and Savannah.

Long-time international travelers Henri and Patricia Safran fell in love with the inn at first sight.

When they purchased it in 2002, they were happy to find access features added by the former owner. Says Henri, "Because of the exterior ramp, guests can enjoy the entire first floor, including the living room, parlor, dining room, and verandah, without encountering any steps. That's a very unique feature in a historic home."

The inn features ramped access from the private parking area at the rear of the building onto a very wide side verandah. The wheelchair-accessible Library Room has direct access to the top of the ramp.

The Library Room has a king-sized bed that can be converted to two smaller beds. The room is decorated in a Victorian theme and is filled with antique oak furniture. A glass-paned French door opens out to the verandah, and there is a second entrance near the fireplace in the living room. The bathroom features a roll-in shower with a hand-held showerhead and a built-in shower bench.

The nightly rates for the Library are $125 for one guest and $145 for two guests.

The Two Suns Inn is just a seven-minute walk from downtown Beaufort. Make sure to stop by the Henry C. Chambers Waterfront Park to get a glimpse of the waterfront at its best. It's a nice place to stroll, or you can just sit and enjoy the water views.

If you'd prefer to hit the beach, Beaufort is just a few minutes from Hilton Head, where many of the beaches offer good access. In fact, Coligny

Beach, Dreissen Beach, Islander's Beach Club, Alder Lane, and Folly Field Beach are all equipped with rubber beach mats to make them wheelchair-accessible. A few of the beaches even have beach wheelchairs for loan. It's a fun place to enjoy the sun and surf.

Two Suns Inn
1705 Bay Street
Beaufort, SC 29902
(843) 522-1122
www.twosunsinn.com

Lampstand B&B

FORT MILL, SOUTH CAROLINA

*B*ill and Mary McGinn built the Lampstand B&B in 1996, on property that's been in their family for over 100 years. Access issues were taken into consideration right from the beginning. Says Mary, "Because I taught special education for a number of years, we tried to design our main house with wheelchairs in mind." Today their comfy log home, which is located on six wooded acres, offers visitors a restful retreat with a casual atmosphere.

There is ramp access to the front porch from the adjacent covered parking area, so guests can park under the carport and wheel right onto the ramp and up to the main house. The first-floor Pleasant Valley Room is located down a wide hallway, just off the living room. Says Mary, "Our goal was to make this room comfortable and workable for almost any guest, without ending up with a sterile, functional-looking environment." And from the looks of it, I'd say they succeeded in spades.

The Pleasant Valley Room is furnished with an antique double bed, a rocking chair, and a low dresser with a tilt mirror. Access features include good pathway access, wide doorways and lowered closet rods. The spacious bathroom has a tub/shower combination with a hand-held showerhead and a grab bar on the back wall. There is also a pedestal sink, a lowered shelf, and a standard-height toilet with a grab bar on the side wall. A toilet riser and a portable shower bench are available upon request.

All of the public areas of the inn, including the dining area, side porch and living room are wheelchair-accessible. Breakfast is served in the dining room or on the deck. Afternoon tea is served in the living room or on one of the porches.

Outside there is a curved ramp leading from the deck down to the garden. The garden paths are covered with pine needles, and most of the herbs and vegetables are in raised beds. It's all nicely accessible; in fact, Mary patterned her garden after the accessible garden at the state botanical garden.

The rate for the Pleasant Valley Room is $65 per night.

The Lampstand B&B features ramped access to the porch. (Photo courtesy of The Lampstand B&B.)

Antiques are a big attraction in the area, and while most of the shops are accessible, some are small and difficult to maneuver through in a wheelchair. Paramount Carowinds, a large theme park with good access, is located nearby. Adds Mary, "We are near NASCAR racing, pro football, and semi-pro baseball. The sporting events have all made modifications for accessibility, so they are a good choice for wheelchair-users."

And last but not least, there is something to be said about the attitude at the Lampstand B&B. Again, Mary and her crew get high marks. "Basically we just want to provide a valuable, enjoyable service to all our guests," she says. "That's the essence of B&Bs anyway; to see each guest as a unique individual with their own special wants and needs, and to find a way to meet those needs whenever possible."

Lampstand B&B
9614 Charlotte Highway
Fort Mill, SC 29715
(803) 547-3100
www.lampstandonline.com

Iron Mountain Inn

BUTLER, TENNESSEE

*L*ocated near Watuga Lake in northeastern Tennessee, the Iron Mountain Inn features four guest rooms plus a detached chalet. To be honest, innkeeper Vicki Woods stumbled upon her innkeeping career. "My late husband and I had entertained a great deal and often had overnight guests," she recalls. "So when he died, it seemed logical to continue doing for money what we had done for fun for many years!"

The main inn does not have any accessible guest rooms as it was built many years ago; however, the newly constructed Creekside Chalet was built from the ground up to be accessible. Says Vicki regarding her decision to

The Creekside Chalet at Iron Mountain Inn features ramped access, an open floor plan and a very spacious deck. (Photo courtesy of Iron Mountain Inn.)

incorporate access features into the chalet, "There are many people who are unable to enjoy the outdoors due to a lack of barrier-free accommodations. As the population ages (me, too) and as more people are willing to try new things, it seemed a logical thing to do."

Vicki refers to the chalet as their "West Wing," as it's located away from the mountaintop inn, nestled between the mountain and a rushing creek. This three-bedroom, fully self-contained cabin features ramp access, an open floor plan, and an accessible bedroom on the first floor. The first-floor bathroom has a roll-in shower. Additionally, the "spa under the stars" is the correct transfer height, but Woods points out that some wheelchair-users may need assistance getting out of the spa.

Breakfast is served in the Great Room of the inn. There are two steps up to the back porch, but Vicki installs a temporary ramp whenever it's needed. In nice weather guests can even enjoy breakfast on the porch.

The rates for the Creekside Chalet range from $150 to $225 per night, depending on the season and the number of people.

As for accessible things to do in the area, it's all about enjoying the great outdoors. "Nearby Watuga Lake is simply beautiful," says Woods. "There are also paved trails suitable for wheelchairs at Roan Mountain State Park. And Sycamore Shoals has a lovely, two-mile-long riverside trail. It's just a beautiful area."

Iron Mountain Inn
138 Moreland Drive
Butler, TN 37640
(423) 768-2446
www.ironmountaininn.com

East Hills B&B

*L*ocated 35 miles west of Nashville, East Hills B&B is billed as a traditional Southern home with over 5,000 square feet of gracious common rooms, porches, and handsomely decorated guest rooms. This stately home, which has been in the Luther family for generations, was constructed in 1940 and fully restored in 1992. Several years later, John and Anita Luther entered the world of innkeeping and welcomed their first guests on May 25, 1995.

John and Anita began with just three guest rooms, but they soon expanded. As Anita recalls, "When we realized we needed to add another bedroom, we both knew we had to make it accessible." Today the property boasts five guest rooms and three cottages, including the accessible Anderson Room.

The front entrance of the home has four steps up to the terrace, another four steps to the porch and two more steps up to the front door. There is a ramped entrance to the enclosed back porch, which is located near the side driveway and parking area. From the back porch there is a short ramp to the Anderson Room on one end, and another short ramp to the living porch, dining area, and living room on the other end.

The oversized Anderson Room is furnished with two queen-sized beds and has plenty of room to maneuver a wheelchair. The bathroom has a roll-under sink, grab bars around the toilet, and a low-step shower with a built-in shower bench. There is a three-inch lip on the shower, but there is plenty of room to transfer to the shower bench. Says Anita, "We've had several wheelchair-users stay in this room and they've all said the bathroom was very accessible."

Guests can access the rest of the house (including the dining room) from the back porch, but breakfast can also be delivered to the Anderson Room on request. The house is located on four acres with level sidewalks and grass-covered paths leading out to the cottages. Sidewalks around the house allow barrier-free access to the gardens and the back patio. These outdoor areas are great places to enjoy the resident bird, squirrel, and rabbit population.

The rate for the Anderson Room is $100 per night.

Many of the stores and restaurants on Main Street are accessible, but the big attraction in Dickson is the Renaissance Center. Say Anita, "The Renaissance Center features a dinner theater, the CyberSphere Theater, the Performing Arts Theater, the Virtually Unlimited Bookstore, and a visual arts gallery. It's very nicely done and the entire building is wheelchair-accessible."

East Hills B&B
100 East Hill Terrace
Dickson, TN 37055
(615) 441-9428
www.easthillsbb.com

Eureka Hotel

*A*lthough this property is technically classified as a hotel, it has a definite B&B feel to it. Indeed, The Eureka Hotel is very homey. In fact, it was originally constructed as a private residence. In 1850 it became known as the Eureka Hotel when it was enlarged and converted to a boarding house. After its heyday, the property fell into disrepair and sat unoccupied for many years. In 1997, six locals with a keen interest in preserving Jonesborough's history formed a partnership and purchased the neglected property. After a massive restoration, the Eureka Hotel reopened on July 1, 2000.

Located in the heart of the historic district, this 15-room hotel is furnished with an equal mix of period antiques and reproductions. In fact, the furnishings and restoration cost an estimated $325 per square foot; mostly because the partners tried to salvage as much as possible from the original property. Today the Eureka Hotel has six ground-floor rooms, including the accessible Mitchell Room. Nine guest rooms are also located on the second floor; however, the hotel lacks an elevator.

When questioned about motivating factors for including an accessible room in this historic property, innkeeper Baxter Bledsoe matter-of-factly replied, "I don't think it ever occurred to any of us not to include an accessible room." He later elaborated on the specifics. "First off, the major investor is a retired orthopedic surgeon," he explained. "He spent a lot of his professional career working with people who use wheelchairs, so he is well aware of accessibility needs. This is also true of my wife, who is a retired RN. Additionally, I was the town building inspector for over five years, so I had a lot of exposure to access issues as well."

The front entrance of the hotel features a wide doorway and a level threshold. The Mitchell Room (also known as Room 111) is the first room on the right. Accessible parking is located around the side of the hotel approximately 80 feet from the front door.

The Mitchell Room pays tribute to the original owner of the building, Robert Mitchell. It is located in the original section of the hotel, which was constructed in 1797. It features wide doorways, level thresholds, and adequate pathway access. The room is furnished with two twin beds and a wheelchair-accessible desk. Access features in the bathroom include a tub/shower combination with a hand-held showerhead, grab bars in the shower and around the toilet, and a roll-under sink.

The Mitchell Room is located directly across from the parlor, where breakfast is served every morning. The parlor is furnished with beautiful antiques, comfortable chairs, and a cozy fireplace. Outside in the back, there is also a garden area and a large brick terrace, which is wheelchair-accessible.

The rate for the Mitchell Room is $129 per night.

The International Storytelling Center is located just one block from the Eureka Hotel. "They have storytellers in residence several weeks between spring and fall," says Baxter. He also recommends Music on the Square, a Friday night street festival that takes place in front of the Storytelling Center. "All of the brick sidewalks here in the historic business district have curb-cuts for wheelchairs," says Baxter. He adds, "As Tennessee's oldest town, Jonesborough is a treasure that everyone should experience."

Eureka Hotel
127 West Main Street
Jonesborough, TN 37659
(423) 913-6100
www.eurekajonesborough.com

Historic Brenham Properties

*L*ocated halfway between Austin and Houston, Brenham is best known as the home of Blue Bell Ice Cream. With a population fast approaching 15,000, Brenham still retains that small-town feel; and indeed the restored Main Street historic district is a very pleasant place to linger. Lingering is a popular pastime throughout town. It's just a great place to decompress and slip away for a few days. In keeping with that small-town ambiance, Brenham boasts a large number of historic B&Bs. two of which offer excellent access.

Far View B&B is billed as a two-acre residential retreat, surrounded by lush gardens, stately trees, and an expansive lawn. This prairie-style home was originally constructed in 1925, and it was designed by Houston architect A.C. Finn. David and Tonya Meyer purchased the property in 1992, and after extensive renovations, they welcomed their first guest in 1994. Even then, the Meyer's renovations were far from over, as they later added two luxury suites in a newly constructed pool house.

Says Tonya, "When we were thinking about adding rooms, our architect suggested that we construct an accessible room as part of the plan for our luxury suites. We wanted our property to be senior-friendly and barrier-free." As a result, Pool House Suite Two was born. At the same time the Meyers added ramp access to the south side of their historic main house.

The pool house addition matches the 1925 main house, with architectural features such as open eaves, keystones, and stained glass windows. Accessible parking is located near the accessible suite, with a paved level walkway leading from the parking area to the door.

Pool House Suite Two features a gas fireplace, a Jacuzzi tub, and a king-sized bed. Access features include wide doorways, level thresholds, and excellent pathway access. The bathroom has a roll-in shower with a built-in shower bench and a hand-held showerhead, a roll-under sink, and grab bars in the shower and around the toilet.

Breakfast is served in the dining room in the main house. With advance notice it can be also delivered to the suite.

The nightly rates for Pool House Suite Two are $167 during the week and $185 on weekends.

Says Tonya, "Our first guests in our accessible room were celebrating their anniversary. They told us that it was so delightful to stay in a wheelchair-accessible luxury room that did not feel like an institutional room."

Another accessible choice, the Ant Street Inn is located just around the corner. This 14-room inn is housed in a 100-year-old commercial building. Even though the renovated building looks more like a hotel than a home, guests consistently give the Ant Street Inn high marks for hospitality, friendliness, and a very homey atmosphere.

"In 2000 we decided to add an additional room," recalls innkeeper Pam Taylor. "Since the main house already had ramp access to the front door, it just made sense to make the new ground-floor guest room wheelchair-accessible."

The accessible San Antonio Room combines Old World charm with New World accessibility. It features wide doorways and level access, and it's decorated with a beamed ceiling, antique Mexican doors, and a queen-sized canopy bed. Special features include a gas fireplace, a wet bar, and a two-person (non-accessible) tub. Large double doors open out to the back porch, which overlooks the garden. "The San Antonio Room is our nicest room," adds Pam.

The bathroom includes a roll-in shower with a hand-held showerhead and grab bars in the shower and around the toilet. The sink has some decorative rails underneath it, but the innkeepers can remove them quickly upon request.

Breakfast is served in the Capital Grill Restaurant, which features ramp access.

The regular rate for the San Antonio room is $235 a night; however, a discounted rate of $165 per night is offered to disabled guests.

Both innkeepers highly recommend the Main Street Historic District, which has been described as the heart and soul of Washington County. Says Pam, "It features a great collection of shops and restaurants, many of which are accessible. Best of all, it's just a short stroll away."

Far View B&B
804 S. Park Street
Brenham, TX 77833
(979) 836-1672
www.farviewbedandbreakfast.com

The Ant Street Inn
107 West Commerce Street
Brenham, TX 77833
(979) 836-7393
www.antstreetinn.com

River Run B&B

Located in the historic section of Kerrville, the River Run B&B takes its name from the Guadalupe River, which runs through the town. This six-room property sports a native stone facade and a high, sloping tin roof; a typical example of the German architecture prevalent throughout Texas hill country.

Inside, innkeepers Ron and Jean Williamson add a bit of their own personalities to the decor, with a hodgepodge of antiques and Texan memorabilia. One of the most interesting pieces is a turn-of-the century pharmacy counter (courtesy of Ron, a retired pharmacist) filled with a display of old-time remedies.

Recalls Ron, "We opened in 1995. I was a hospital pharmacist and Jean was a nurse administrator, so it was very important to us to be able to serve all guests, including those with disabilities."

The River Run B&B features ramp access to the front porch and a level threshold at the front door. Accessible parking is located approximately 10 feet from the ramp. The accessible Leander McNelly Room has an outside entrance from the porch as well as an interior entrance from the great room, both of which have wide doorways and level thresholds.

The Leander McNelly Room is named after a famous Texas Ranger who is well known for making the area safe from bandits and renegade Indians. It features a queen-sized bed, hardwood floors, and adequate pathway access. The bathroom includes a marble (non-accessible) whirlpool tub, a large roll-in shower with a portable shower chair, grab bars around the toilet and in the shower, and a roll-under sink.

The first-floor public areas, including the great room, several porches, and the dining room, feature barrier-free access. The library is located on the second floor and is only accessible by a flight of stairs.

The nightly rate for the Leander McNelly Room is $105.

The River Run B&B is conveniently located next door to the Riverside Nature Center, which features level access to the visitors' center and an accessible nature trail. Says Ron, "Some of our other nature trails are also wheelchair-accessible. Additionally, we have two very fine live theaters in town that do excellent productions. Both are wheelchair-accessible."

"We've had guests from all over Texas, 19 states, and 15 different foreign countries stay at our inn," adds Ron proudly. "And they all left with a smile on their face."

River Run B&B
120 Francisco Lemos Street
Kerrville, TX 78028
(830) 896-8353
www.riverrunbb.com

Almost HeavInn

L ocated in the heart of scenic East Texas, Almost HeavInn is a quiet retreat situated on 35 acres recently designated as a Backyard Wildlife Habitat by the National Wildlife Federation. The grounds include a small pond, a number of walking paths, and of course a lot of wildlife.

As the property name implies, innkeepers Dwight and Carol Omenson have a religious background, although the inn is not strictly billed as a religious retreat. Still, if you are not comfortable with Bible verses and cherubs, this might not be a good choice for you.

Before building the five-room inn in 2002, Dwight was a firefighter and Carol worked in a church office. The Omensons seem genuinely concerned with access, and in fact it was on their minds before construction ever began on the inn. Says Carol, "We have a friend who has ALS, and when we were building we planned our downstairs bedroom to be wheelchair-accessible in hopes that he would be able to visit us."

The front porch of the inn is accessible from the nearby driveway; however, there is a four-inch step up into the house. The first-floor Kinkaid Room is flagged as wheelchair-accessible, but because of a few steps and other access obstacles it's really best suited for a slow walker or a wheelchair-user who can walk a few steps. Still, the Omensons are very welcoming hosts, so their attitude should factor into the whole access equation. The bottom line is, this property is not 100% barrier-free, but many wheelchair-users will be very comfortable there.

The Kinkaid Room features a king-sized bed, two wingback recliners, and adequate room to maneuver a wheelchair. The oversized shower has a small lip, so technically it is not a roll-in; however, many wheelchair-users will be able to transfer to the built-in shower seat. The shower also has a hand-held showerhead and grab bars.

As far as public rooms go, the first-floor dining room and guest leisure room have good pathway access, but the back porch has a four-inch step.

The nightly rates for the Kinkaid Room range from $95 to $110. The lowest rates are available during the week.

The biggest attraction in the area is the Texas State Railroad, a vintage steam train that travels between Rusk and Palestine. All trains are wheelchair-accessible, and each train has one wheelchair-accessible restroom. It's truly a must-see for train buffs.

But if you'd rather just kick back and relax at Almost HeavInn, that's okay too. Says Carol, "Many people visit us because they desire a quiet and peaceful retreat, and they have a wonderful time here."

Almost HeavInn
RR 4, Box 14701
Rusk, TX 75785
(903) 795-3181
www.almostheavinn.com

Christmas House B&B

SAN ANTONIO, TEXAS

*P*enny Estes invites everyone to enjoy Christmas year round at her appropriately named Christmas House B&B in San Antonio, Texas. Housed in a quaint 1908 two-story home, this five-room property is adorned with festive artwork and holiday decorations, most of which are for sale. This B&B, complete with a Christmas tree in the parlor, is designed to get you in a holiday mood by sampling a little bit of the Christmas spirit 365 days a year.

As you can imagine, Penny is a big Christmas fan. She opened her B&B in 1997, and Christmas just seemed a natural theme. Lest you think Penny had her head in the clouds in the design phase, rest assured she put some serious thought into access issues before she opened her doors.

The Christmas House B&B is just a few miles from the RiverWalk,
which features wheelchair-access to 75% of the paths.

"I've done a lot of work with disabled students, as I was a teacher and I'm now a high school counselor," says Penny. "My mother is in her nineties and access became a big concern so she could come and stay with us on holidays.

To that end, we made sure we included ramp access to our house and an accessible ground-floor guest room when we opened the B&B," says Penny. Hence the Blue and Silver Room was created.

The Blue and Silver Room features an armoire, dresser, and king-sized bed with a handmade Amish quilt. There is good pathway access throughout the room. Access features in the oversized bathroom include a roll-in shower with a fold-down shower seat, grab bars by the toilet, and a roll-under sink

The entire downstairs area, including the living room, dining room, and back verandah, also features barrier-free access.

The rates for the Blue and Silver Room are $85 per night on weekends and $75 per night during the week.

The Christmas House B&B is located just a few miles from the River-Walk, where you'll find a bevy of shops, restaurants, and galleries. Billed as one of the most visited places in Texas, this pedestrian-friendly walkway was originally constructed in 1933, but thanks to local advocacy efforts it's now approximately 75% accessible. The City of San Antonio Disability Access Office publishes an excellent RiverWalk access map. Copies of the access map are also posted along the RiverWalk.

No matter what you do, it's hard not to enjoy San Antonio. The friendly locals, like Penny Estes, really make you feel at home. Indeed, they even make you want to come back again. Penny sums it up best with her words and her attitude. "We enjoy people and are very proud of our town and our establishment," she cheerfully declares.

Christmas House B&B
2307 McCullough
San Antonio, TX 78212
(210) 737-2786
www.christmashousebnb.com

Vieh's B&B

*L*ocated in a five-acre palm grove in southeast Texas, Vieh's B&B is billed as a ranch-style home with a Mexican flavor. Innkeepers Charles and Lana Vieh first started charging for rooms in 1994 for some extra income. They soon discovered they really liked being innkeepers and enjoyed their guests, so they decided to give it a go full-time. Today Vieh's B&B has five guest rooms and one cottage, and a very homey atmosphere that makes guests feel like old friends.

The accessibility at Vieh's B&B evolved over a number of years. Says Charles, "My mother moved in with us and she need an accessible room with a roll-in shower, so of course we built one for her. It later became our Mama Grande Room."

The entire house is on a single level, and parking is located approximately 30 feet from the front door, There is one step up to the front door, but the Viehs can quickly set up their portable ramp if it is needed.

The 20' x 22' Mama Grande room features a private entrance and a sitting area. It is furnished with a queen-sized bed, a microwave and a small refrigerator. Access features include wide doorways, level thresholds, and good pathway access. The bathroom has a 4' x5' roll-in shower with grab bars, and grab bars around the toilet.

All of the public areas, including the breakfast area, have good pathway access and level thresholds. Outside there is a large landscaped garden and a paved patio and walkway. There is also a gazebo on a lake at the back of the property, which can be reached by car.

The rate for the Mama Grande Room is $95 per night.

The big attraction of this area is its diverse natural beauty. It's also a prime birding venue. Says Charles, "We have a number of wildlife parks in our area and a nice little birding trail around our own private lake."

Vieh's B&B is located just nine miles form the Laguna Atascosa National Wildlife Refuge in Rio Honda. This refuge features a number of accessible trails, including the Paisano Trail, the Butterfly Garden Walk, the Kiskadee Trail, and the Alligator Pond Trail. There are also two driving routes through the refuge, an accessible birdfeeding station and photo blind, an accessible scope at the Osprey Overlook, and an accessible viewing platform on Alligator Pond. It's a great place to spend the day and enjoy Mother Nature.

Vieh's B&B
18413 Landrum Park Road
San Benito, TX 78586
(956) 425-4651
www.vieh.com

*The accessible Kiskadee Trail at Laguna Atascosa
National Wildlife Refuge in Rio Honda.*

Casa de Siesta

SOUTH PADRE ISLAND, TEXAS

As you stroll through Casa de Siesta's quiet courtyard, you just want to sit down, put up your feet, close your eyes, and nod off for a few hours. Indeed, the atmosphere is just as relaxing as the name implies. Even though this 12-room inn is located on South Padre's main drag, it's one of the few places that's unscathed by the spring-break masses. And believe me, that's a very good thing!

Although local codes dictated the inclusion of an accessible room when the property was constructed in 2000, innkeepers Ron and Lynn Speier thought it was a great idea right from the start. Says Lynn, "Actually we wanted the rooms to be easily accessible to everyone. I for one do not like large hotel properties, where you have to walk for what seems like blocks just to get to your room. It's all very tiring."

But you won't find that at Casa de Siesta, as the ground floor rooms are all located around a central courtyard. Accessible parking is located near the front entrance, and there is a barrier-free pathway from the parking area, around the courtyard to the office in the back of the property.

The accessible Capistrano Room is just a short distance from the office. Access features include wide doorways, excellent pathway access, and tile floors. The room is furnished with two double beds, a desk, and a refrigerator. It should be noted that the furniture is all pretty massive and the beds are 31 inches high. The bathroom has a beautiful tile roll-in shower with a hand-held showerhead, grab bars in the shower and around the toilet, a roll-under sink and an enlarged dressing area. A portable shower chair is available upon request.

There is level access to the pathway around the courtyard and to the inside dining area. There are two steps down to the courtyard and pool area, but Lynn says that they can construct some type of portable ramp should the need arise. "To be honest," she says, "nobody has ever asked for that before, but it is something we can do."

The very spacious Capistrano Room at Casa de Siesta.

The nightly rate for the Capistrano Room ranges from $99 to $150. The highest rates are during the holidays and in the summer.

There are plenty of accessible things to do on the island. For starters you can take the free, accessible Wave shuttle around the island or to the beach. There is boardwalk access to the beach, and beach mats over the sand at beach access points 6 and 16, just off of Gulf Boulevard. And don't miss the nicely accessible Laguna Madre Boardwalk, next to the convention center. It's a great place to spot birds, butterflies, and even alligators.

Of course, you could also just sit back and do nothing. And Casa de Siesta is the perfect place to do just that.

Casa de Siesta
4610 Padre Boulevard
South Padre Island, TX 78957
(956) 761-5656
www.casadesiesta.com

Castle Valley Inn

CASTLE VALLEY, UTAH

*L*ocated just outside of Moab, the Castle Valley Inn is the only lodging establishment in the tiny bedroom community of Castle Valley. It's close to the natural beauty of Utah, yet far away from the hubbub of busy Moab. Nestled among five acres of carefully tended orchards, lawns, and fields, the Castle Valley Inn is a true retreat in every sense of the word.

This 11-room inn includes three cabins and eight guest rooms. Innkeeper Hertha Wakefield is astutely aware of access issues from her own experience. To that end, she recently remodeled the Anasazi Cabin to accommodate wheelchair-users. Says Hertha, "We have had the opportunity to take care of the elders in our two families and have traveled with them. As my husband and I get older we understand their unique needs for travel. When the opportunity arose for us to upgrade our rooms, we wanted to include access in the plan. It not only makes our property more marketable, but our guests with mobility disabilities really appreciate it."

The Anasazi Cabin features a ramped entrance, wide doorways, level thresholds, and excellent pathway access. The cabin is furnished with a queen-sized bed in one room and a bunkbed in another room. It also includes a small kitchenette, a wraparound porch, and an outdoor gas grill. And the views of Castle Rock and Parriott Mesa from this cabin are simply stunning.

The bathroom has a low-step shower (with a four-inch lip) with a handheld showerhead. A sturdy shower chair is also available. Additionally, lever-type doorknobs and faucets have been installed throughout the cabin.

The smaller Fremont Bungalow also has level access; however, it lacks the accessible bathroom adaptations present in the Anasazi Cabin. It has one queen-sized bed and a kitchenette. This cabin may be suitable for some slow walkers, primarily because of the zero-step entrance. Says Hertha, "The Anasazi Cabin is the most accessible choice, but we've had many wheelchair-users stay in the Fremont Bungalow, too."

There are eight steps at the entrance of the main house and three steps to the outdoor dining patio. Breakfast can be delivered to the cabins upon request.

The rate for the Anasazi Cabin is $175 per night, and the rate for the Fremont Bungalow is $160 per night.

The area around Moab is some of the most beautiful on earth. Says Hertha, "Windshield touring is the most popular activity for soft adventurers. There is also a wheelchair-accessible chairlift to the top of the Moab Rim. From the top you get a spectacular view the Moab Valley, Arches National Park, and the western portal of the Colorado River Gorge."

Hertha also suggests a visit to Arches National Park. "It's a great park to drive through with most of the major features visible from the car," she says. "There is also a good wheelchair-accessible overlook in the Islands of the Sky District in Canyonlands National Park. The Moab area offers something for everyone who enjoys nature."

Castle Valley Inn
HC64 Box 2602
Moab, UT 84532
(435) 259-6012
www.castlevalleyinn.com

West Mountain Inn

ARLINGTON, VERMONT

Nestled on a mountainside in southwestern Vermont, the West Mountain Inn is just a four-hour drive away from New York City or Boston. In fact I first learned about this property from my New York City–based publisher.

Originally constructed in 1894, this seven-gabled farmhouse was converted to an elegant estate in 1924. Over 50 years later it underwent yet another metamorphosis, when Mary Ann and Wes Carlson purchased the property and converted it to a 20-room country inn. Today the West Mountain Inn is billed as a space to relax and rejuvenate the body and the spirit.

After Wes passed away in 2000, daughter Amie Emmons returned from California to help her mom run the inn. As Amie points out, access at the inn was very important to her parents from day one. "My grandfather had polio when he was in his early 30s, and he spent the rest of his life in a wheelchair," recalls Amie. "When my parents bought the inn, one of the first additions they made was to put in an accessible guest room on the main floor and make all of the common rooms accessible so that he and other disabled guests could come and visit comfortably."

The front entrance of the inn features a zero-step walkway, a level threshold, and a wide doorway. Gwendolyn's Room is located on the first floor, just off of the game room, and it's furnished with a king-sized bed and a remote-controlled gas fireplace. There is plenty of room to wheel around in this spacious room, which also features a great view of the bird feeders and the back lawn. Access features in the bathroom include a roll-in shower with a hand-held showerhead, grab bars in the shower and around the toilet, lever faucets, and a roll-under sink. A portable shower chair is available upon request.

All of the first-floor common rooms, including the living room, bar, game room, dining room, and public bathrooms, are wheelchair-accessible. The inn is surrounded by lawns that are fairly level and are usually accessible in good weather.

The nightly rate for Gwendolyn's Room ranges from $149 to $304. The highest rates are on weekends during the fall.

Southwestern Vermont is known for it's many cultural and historical attractions. Amie recommends the Southern Vermont Art Center, the Bennington Museum, the Norman Rockwell Gallery, and the Mass MoCA.

Adds Amie, "We have many disabled guests who come back to us year after year because of our friendliness and willingness to make sure they have the best experience possible!"

West Mountain Inn
River Road
Arlington, VT 05250
(802) 375-6516
www.westmountaininn.com

Sinclair Inn

*B*uilt in 1890, the Sinclair Inn was originally the home of Edmund and Ruth Sinclair. In 1913 the local hotel burned down, and the Sinclairs opened their home to paying guests. In the 1950s this Queen Anne Victorian home was converted into a home for elderly women, and in the late 1980s it became a traditional B&B. Today the Sinclair Inn continues to welcome guests, and thanks to access improvements over the years, this historic inn is nicely accessible.

In fact, access is why former owner Nancy Ames purchased the property. Says Ames, "My mother has multiple sclerosis; therefore, I made access one of my criteria in purchasing the right property." Today the access remains excellent at the six-room Sinclair Inn, with new owners Sally and Bruce Gilbert-Smith at the helm.

There is ramp access to the front door of the inn. The accessible room (Room 1) is located on the first floor and has four large windows that overlook the lovely garden. The room features a king-sized bed that can be converted into two twins, a comfortable sitting area, and an oversized bathroom. The bathroom has a roll-in shower with grab bars, a hand-held showerhead, and a fold-down shower seat.

The living room and parlor both offer barrier-free access. Breakfast is served in the accessible dining room, which is located on the first floor. Guests can access the 15,000-square-foot Victorian garden from the front lawn. The garden features a 30-foot pond, a cascading waterfall, and a pathway that winds through myriad plants, shrubs, birches, and evergreen trees.

The nightly rates for Room 1 range from $100 to $160 per night, with the lowest rates in the winter.

Local sites of interest include numerous antique shops and small museums, Ben & Jerry's Ice Cream Factory, and Shelburne Farms. Additionally, the shops and restaurants of downtown Burlington are just a short drive away. And if you're planning ahead for a winter break, be sure to check out the adaptive skiing program at Sugarbush Resort in Warren, which is located just an hour's drive from the inn.

Sinclair Inn
389 Vermont Route 15
Jericho, VT 05465
(802) 899-2234
www.sinclairinnbb.com

Russell Young Farm B&B

*I*nnkeepers Carol and Dennis Hysko had a lot of work in front of them when they purchased the Russell Young Farm in 1997. Located on 70 acres of woodlands and pastures, this 1800s farmhouse has seen many incarnations; from a dairy farm, to a ski lodge, to a family vacation home. After extensive renovations, the Hyskos gave it yet another life as a country B&B as they welcomed their first guests in September 2003.

The decision to make their property wheelchair-accessible was heavily influenced by the Hyskos personal experience. "Before we moved to Vermont, Carol had a serious injury on a horse, and she had to use a walker and could not climb stairs for three months," says Dennis. "When we came to Vermont to look for property, we were unable to find lodging that was accessible because of her walker. We decided right then and there that if we ever owned a B&B we would make it accessible."

The three-room property features a level entrance, with a gentle incline leading up to the house from the nearby parking lot. The accessible Shalmansir Room is located on the first floor.

The Shalmansir Room has a private entrance with a wide doorway and a level threshold. The bathroom features a roll-in shower with a handheld showerhead, grab bars in the shower and around the toilet, and a roll-under sink with a tiltable mirror. A portable shower bench is available upon request.

The Hyskos even remembered the small details, such as lowered clothing rods in the closet and wheelchair-height hooks on the back of the bathroom door. It's obvious that a good deal of thought went into the accessible design of this room.

The entire first floor of the house, including the front porch, the great room, and the dining area, is accessible from the Shalmansir Room. "The front porch is ideal for magnificent views of the Green Mountains," says Dennis. "We also have three horses and one donkey for viewing."

The rate for the Shalmansir Room is $125 per night.

As for things to do in the area, Dennis says "We're within 45 minutes of the Shelburne Museum, Shelburne Farms, Middlebury College, and the University of Vermont. It's really a great place to relax and enjoy the beautiful scenery Vermont has to offer."

Russell Young Farm B&B
861 Russell Young Road
Jerusalem, VT 05443
(802) 453-7026
www.russellyoungfarm.com

Rabbit Hill Inn

LOWER WATERFORD, VERMONT

*I*f you're looking for a romantic getaway, the Rabbit Hill Inn is just what the doctor ordered. In fact, I first learned about this property after a friend spent a very romantic 25th-anniversary weekend there. She talked about it for weeks. Maybe it's the location of the inn, or maybe it's just the little extras that innkeepers Brian and Leslie Mulcahy provide. No matter the reason, this property definitely gets high marks for romantic ambiance as well as accessibility.

Says Brain, "We were lucky because the previous owners added the barrier-free room when they made some additions to the property. I believe it was required under the code. In any case, the room was already on-line when we purchased the property in 1994."

There are fours steps up to the front porch of the main house; however, a ramped entrance is available on the side of the building. Parking is available approximately 30 feet from the accessible entrance. A level pathway leads from the parking area to the accessible entrance.

The wheelchair-accessible Turnabout Room is located on the ground level of the 1795 Tavern Building. It has a small porch and a private entrance with a wide doorway and a level threshold. This luxury room is furnished with a king-sized canopy bed, and it includes a gas fireplace in the sitting area and a (non-accessible) whirlpool tub in the bathroom. There is good pathway access throughout the spacious room, and little features such as lowered closet rods really help make it more useable.

Access features in the bathroom include an oversized roll-in shower with a hand-held showerhead and a fold-down shower seat, grab bars in the shower and around the toilet, a raised toilet, and a roll-under sink.

All of the first-floor public areas of the main house, including the dining room and the parlors, are wheelchair-accessible. Access features include wide doorways, level thresholds, and good pathway access.

The rates for the Turnabout Room range from $295 to $310 per night.

As for things to do in the area, Brain recommends enjoying the beautiful scenery of northeastern Vermont. "We are just 20 minutes north of Franconia Notch State Park, which has a number of wheelchair-accessible walks and trails," says Brian. "To be honest though, most people come up here for a romantic escape. Our location is very conducive to romance and relaxation."

Rabbit Hill Inn
48 Lower Waterford Road
Lower Waterford, VT 05848
(802) 748-5168
www.rabbithillinn.com

The Inn at Ormsby Hill

MANCHESTER CENTER, VERMONT

The building that houses the Inn at Ormsby Hill has a long and colorful history behind it. Originally constructed in 1794 by Thompson Purdy, this manor house later became the home of prominent Chicago attorney Edward Isham. After a brief stint as a country retreat for underprivileged city boys, the property was abandoned until it was converted to a five-room inn in 1987. When Ted and Chris Sprague purchased the property in 1995, they added five more guest rooms and made the inn accessible.

Says Ted, "When we purchased the inn we decided to make the Library Room wheelchair-accessible. To do that, we completely redid the bathroom and widened two doorways. The doorways had beams from the 1760s so it was quite a challenge!"

The ground-floor Library Room is located just off the gathering room. In the 1800s it was Edward Isham's personal library. Most of the books that line the shelves, including some first editions, are from his private collection. Access features in the Library Room include excellent pathway access and a spacious bathroom with a roll-in shower, built-in shower bench and a hand-held showerhead.

All of the first-floor public areas feature level thresholds and barrier-free access, including the living room, gathering room, and conservatory. "We also put in a new marble walk leading to the front door," adds Ted. "In the end, we dropped the floor to make the house completely accessible without taking away from the historic nature of the building."

The rates for the Library range from $225 to $340 per night.

Nearby Manchester offers a plethora of accessible tourism options. Says Ted, "Our guests go there to enjoy summer theater, outlet shops, art galleries, and concerts. Many of the venues and shops are wheel-chair-accessible."

Adds Ted, "Everyone who has stayed in the Library Room in a wheel-chair has been absolutely thrilled, including one couple who have come back four times. He uses a wheelchair, and he told me that they usually don't find such luxury or elegance in an accessible room."

The Inn at Ormsby Hill
1842 Main Street
Manchester Center, VT 05255
(802) 362-1163
www.ormsbyhill.com

Golden Stage Inn

*I*nnkeeper Sandy Gregg describes her Golden Stage Inn as "an antique-filled, country inn with an atmosphere of relaxed elegance." Located in the heart of Vermont, this 10-room inn has served many purposes throughout its life; first as a 1788 stagecoach stop, then as an Underground Railroad haven, and finally as the home of theater performer Otis Skinner. It had been an inn for almost 40 years when Sandy and Peter Gregg took over the helm in 1999.

Says Sandy, "When we were doing our inn search and found that the Golden Stage Inn was the only historic inn in the greater Okemo Valley area with true wheelchair accessibility, we were thrilled."

Many access upgrades, including ramp access to the entrance and the wide wraparound front porch, were made to this Proctorsville inn by former owners Micki and Paul Darnaurer. Accessible parking is located near the entrance with barrier-free access to the front door via a wide, level sidewalk. Maya's Room (9) is wheelchair-accessible.

This first-floor room was named for Maya Angelou, and it reflects the era when the house was a stop on the Underground Railroad. It has a queen-sized bed, a private bathroom, and a TV. Access features include a level threshold, wide doorways, wooden floors, and good pathway access.

Access to the bathroom is via a wide pocket door. The bathroom has a large roll-in shower with a fold-down shower seat and a hand-held showerhead. There are grab bars on three sides of the shower, and the soap dispenser is lowered for easy access. Other access features include a roll-under sink and grab bars around the toilet.

Most of the public areas, including the colonial dining room, the main parlor, and the fireside room, have barrier-free access. The solarium dining room has a two-inch threshold. There is level access to the garden area and the pool deck.

The rates for Maya's Room range from $79 to $330, with many package deals and seasonal specials available.

Sandy is full of sightseeing suggestions for her guests. "Weston Playhouse, Fletcher Farm School for the Arts & Crafts, and Okemo Mountain Resort are some of the big attractions in our area," she says. "Calvin Coolidge Homestead is a personal favorite of mine, and it's only a 20-minute drive up scenic Route 100 in Plymouth Notch."

Golden Stage Inn
399 Depot Street
Proctorsville, VT 05153
(802) 226-7744
www.goldenstageinn.com

Nellysford Favorites

NELLYSFORD, VIRGINIA

Nestled in the foothills of the majestic Blue Ridge Mountains, two Central Virginia properties offer visitors a definite choice in accessible lodging. Although both properties feature good access, each has a unique flavor. The Mark Addy welcomes visitors with its refined Victorian charm, while the Acorn Inn just oozes a down-home country flavor. Indeed, variety is the spice of life in Nellysford.

The beautifully restored Mark Addy Inn beckons visitors to enjoy the romance and richness of a bygone era. This historic home was once the residence of Dr. John C. Everett, but today innkeeper John Maddox welcomes guests to his beautifully restored nine-room inn.

John is surprisingly candid about his motivation for making his property accessible. "To be honest, initially I was required to provide access when we renovated the property; however, once I discovered that very few properties in our area were accessible, I took it a step further and went beyond the minimum requirements," John recalls. "I figured we could attract a whole new market of travelers if we had the facilities they needed."

John's access improvements include ramp access to the front verandah of the property. The front entrance of the inn is only accessible by stairs, but a concrete pathway leads from the accessible parking area to a ramp just outside the accessible Lillemor Room.

The Lillemor Room was named for one of John's relatives, and it means "little mother" in Swedish. Access features include wide doorways and good pathway access throughout the room. The bathroom has a spacious roll-in shower with a fold-down shower seat.

All of the first-floor public rooms feature barrier-free access. Breakfast is served in the dining room. Adds John, "Last weekend we had a guest in a wheelchair who chose to stay in another first-floor room that we don't consider wheelchair-accessible. She had no problems with the space and she certainly enjoyed several of our numerous porches."

The rates for the Lillemor Room range from $110 to $125 per night.

Down the road, innkeepers Kathy and Martin Versluys welcome visitors to their decidedly country Acorn Inn. This European-style property features 10 rooms housed in a converted horse barn, two guest rooms in the main house, and one self-contained cottage. The horse-barn guest rooms (housed in a building called "the inn") all feature barrier-free access.

Kathy and Martin renovated the property in 1987 and converted the horse barn to guest rooms. Says Kathy, "To be honest, the horse barn with its wide corridor and stall doors really lent itself generously to being accessible."

The horse-barn building features a zero-step entrance with accessible parking available just 10 feet from the front door. Although the gravel-covered parking lot is not the ideal choice for wheelchair-users, its proximity to the front door makes it a doable option for many people.

All 10 guest rooms in the converted horse barn have wide doorways, and they each measure 12 feet square. Each room is furnished with a double bed, a desk, a side table, and a wardrobe. Pathway access is good in the rooms; however, the innkeepers will remove the desk if more space is needed to access the far side of the bed.

The shared community bathrooms also have numerous access features. If you'd like more privacy in the bathroom, it's possible to go in and simply lock the door. Each bathroom (men's and women's) features one low-step shower with a built-in shower seat and a hand-held showerhead, a raised toilet, grab bars in the shower and around the toilet, and a roll-under sink.

The rates for the horse-barn rooms range from $42 to $57 per night. The lowest rates are available on weekdays.

As far as accessible activities in the area are concerned, both innkeepers agree that the biggest attraction is the scenic beauty of Blue Ridge Mountains. During the spring, summer, and fall, the nearby Blue Ridge Parkway is an excellent choice for a driving tour. Adds Kathy, "The Wintergreen Ski Resort is just 12 miles away. The resort has an adaptive ski program, so it's a great choice for accessible winter recreation."

Mark Addy Inn
56 Rodes Farm Drive
Nellysford, VA 22958
(434) 361-1101
www.mark-addy.com

Acorn Inn
P.O. Box 431
Nellysford, VA 22958
(434) 361-9357
www.acorninn.com

GrandView B&B

*L*ocated on Chesapeake Bay, this four-room B&B is nestled on a peninsula at the mouth of the Great Wicomico River. Every room has an water view; in fact, the inn takes its name from that "grand view" of the bay.

Truth be told, that grand view is what first attracted innkeepers Chris and Sandye Mills to the area. They visited Reedville after attending a conference in Washington, D.C., and they immediately realized it was the place they wanted to live. So in 2000, they retired, relocated from Vancouver, and built the GrandView B&B.

Says Chris, "Sandye has multiple sclerosis, so when we built the house we combined our need for accessibility with our desire to operate a B&B. We chose a builder who could incorporate universal design features into our home, yet allowed us some flexibility with the floor plan." Sandye and Chris welcomed their first guests to the GrandView B&B in Spring, 2001.

Access features of the property include ramp access to the porch, level thresholds, wide doorways, lever hardware, and an open floor plan. Accessible parking is available in the back of the house. Both of the ground-floor guest rooms, the Sisters Room and the Quilt Room, are wheelchair-accessible.

Access features in the ground-floor rooms include wide doorways and good pathway access. The Sisters Room has a queen-sized bed and a private deck, while the Quilt Room has a full-sized bed. Chris is happy to remove furniture from either room, should the need arise.

The ground-floor guest rooms share a hall bathroom, which has a tub/shower combination with a hand-held showerhead and a bench seat. Says Sandye, "If somebody needs a roll-in shower, we can make arrangements for them to use the one in our master suite."

All of the ground-floor public areas, including the foyer, dining room, and front and rear decks, feature barrier-free access. The yard is level and fairly easy to navigate in a wheelchair. Sandye and Chris also have plans to construct an accessible boardwalk to the private pier.

The Sisters Room rents for $90 per night, and the Quilt Room rents for $80 per night.

Reedville is sometimes described as a miniature Cape May, boasting a Main Street lined with stately Victorian mansions. It's just two hours from Richmond and a little over an hour from Williamsburg, so it makes a good base for exploring the historic attractions in the area. Adds Chris, "We also have a first-class Fisherman's Museum downtown. It's wheelchair-accessible and it's a great way to learn about local history."

GrandView B&B
114 Riverside Lnne
Reedville, VA 22539
(804) 453-3890
www.grandviewbb.freeyellow.com

The Grey Horse Inn

T he Grey Horse Inn is located in a part of northern Virginia that remains untouched by urban sprawl, yet is close enough to the urban
centers of Washington, D.C., and Baltimore. Nestled between Middleburg
and Warrenton, this six-room inn is the perfect choice for a romantic holiday
or a weekend getaway.

John and Ellen Hearty purchased the property in April 2001. Says John,
"The inn was already barrier-free when we bought it, but I'm glad that we are
able to serve a wide variety of guests."

There is level access to the porch from the front driveway and a small
one-inch threshold at the front door. The front entrance is used to access the
upstairs bedrooms, the dining room, and the gathering rooms. The accessible Piedmont Room is located around the corner on the basement level,
and it has a private entrance. Accessible parking is located about 30 feet from
the Piedmont Room, with a level walkway leading from the parking area to
the room.

The Piedmont Room features a king-sized bed, wide doorways, level
thresholds, and good pathway access. The bathroom has a low-step shower
with a hand-held showerhead, a portable shower bench, and grab bars in
the shower and around the toilet. This very private garden room opens out
to a large garden filled with grass and gravel walkways, some of which are
wheelchair-accessible.

The gathering rooms and dining room are accessible through the front
entrance, which is located up a slight incline on the other side of the house.
The Piedmont Room includes a table and chairs for guests who prefer in-
room dining. Alternatively, breakfast can be served in the garden.

Nightly rates for the Piedmont Room range from $105 to $155.

For the horse-lover, nearby Great Meadow and Glenwood Park offer steeplechase racing, polo, and other equestrian events, including the

Virginia Gold Cup and International Gold Cup. These events all have accessible seating.

Adds John, "Warrenton is just 15 minutes from the inn. There is a paved Rails to Trails pathway there, which has good wheelchair access. It's a great place to enjoy the outdoors."

The Grey Horse Inn
4350 Fauquier Avenue
The Plains, VA 20198
(540) 253-7000
www.greyhorseinn.com

Long Hill B&B

WINCHESTER, VIRGINIA

The Long Hill B&B is situated in the middle of 19 woodland acres at the northern end of Virgina's Shenandoah Valley. Originally constructed as a private residence, the home was built with antique materials salvaged from log homes in the area. The result is a building that blends in beautifully with the natural surroundings. Today this three-room B&B is a great place to enjoy nature and get away from it all.

Innkeeper Rhoda Kriz was concerned about access long before construction ever began on the Long Hill B&B. After sustaining a hip fracture in her twenties, she learned a lot about access issues while recovering on crutches. Fearing decreased mobility as she ages, Rhoda designed her house with at least one zero-step path to all areas. Says Rhoda, "I don't know if I will always be able to climb stairs, so I want to make sure my home is accessible to me when I get older." The wheelchair access has already been put to the test. Recalls Rhoda, "My mother was in a wheelchair when she lived with us, and she was able to navigate everywhere she needed to go in the house."

The back entrance features zero-step access from the patio, through a wide sliding-glass door. Accessible parking is located approximately 75 feet from the back door. Two of the ground-floor guest rooms, the Azalea Room and the Apple Blossom Room, are wheelchair-accessible.

The Azalea Room is the closest room to the accessible entrance. It features wide doorways and good pathway access. The bathroom has a standard shower with grab bars, a hand-held showerhead, and a built-in shower seat. Other access features include a raised toilet and a roll-under sink. The Apple Blossom Room has identical access features, but it's located farther from the accessible entrance.

All of the ground-floor public areas are wheelchair-accessible through wide double doors that lead to the dining room, library, and kitchen. Out back, there is level access to the stone patio, and the bird and butterfly garden is just 100 feet from the patio. There is also level access to the recreation room from outside.

The Azalea Room and the Apple Blossom Room each rent for $95 per night.

As far as accessible activities in the area are concerned, Rhoda recommends attending a performance at Shenandoah University or browsing through the old town pedestrian mall. "They are both wheelchair-accessible," she says. "Actually the best time to visit Winchester is during our spring apple blossom festival or our fall apple harvest festival as there are a lots of special activities during those times."

Long Hill B&B
547 Apple Pie Ridge Road
Winchester, VA 22603
(540) 450-0341
www.longhillbb.com

Saratoga Inn

LANGLEY, WASHINGTON

*L*ocated on Whidbey Island in Puget Sound, the Saratoga Inn was constructed in 1994, but architecturally it's reminiscent of the early 1900s. This gable-roofed 15-room inn includes a large wraparound porch, lots of warm wood in the interior, and gas fireplaces in every guest room.

Room 4 was designed to be accessible, and to be honest that's why it's such a great room. Everything in it works access-wise. Says innkeeper Cheryl Lambour, "We've had many wheelchair-users stay in this room and they have all been pleased with the access features." Cheryl has a real sensitivity about access issues, as her mother is in a wheelchair. It's nice to have a host who understands.

The Saratoga Inn gets high marks for physical access as well as attitude. There is an accessible parking space in the small parking lot behind the inn, and ramped access to the porch. The front door has a level threshold and a wide doorway.

Room 4 is located on the first floor, just off the front lobby. It has a large fireplace, two big windows, and private access to the wraparound porch. The view of the water is great from this corner room.

The spacious bathroom has a five-foot turning radius and features a roll-in shower with a hand-held showerhead, grab bars, and a portable plastic shower seat. There are grab bars by the toilet and lever handles, a lowered mirror, and a roll-under sink in the bathroom.

There is plenty of room to maneuver a wheelchair in the guest room, and there is barrier-free access to all of the first-floor public rooms. Generally speaking, the property is very nicely done access-wise.

Nightly rates for Room 4 range from $110 to $165, depending on the day of the week and the season. The highest rates are for Saturday nights in the summer.

Getting to Whidbey Island is easy. Just take the Washington State Ferry from Mukilteo, approximately 30 minutes north of Seattle. It's a short ride, and you don't even have to get out of your car. The ferry docks at Clinton on Whidbey Island, and from there it's only a 12-minute drive to the Saratoga Inn.

As for things to do on Whidbey Island, the Edgecliff Restaurant is located right down the street from the inn, and it has an accessible dining room with a great view. It's a great place have a leisurely Sunday brunch. Cheryl recommends taking a driving tour of the island and seeing the Greenbake Farm & Winery, Coupville, and Deception Pass. But, she admits, "the best thing to do here is to relax. The favorite activity around the inn is stretching out on the porch and enjoying a good book. People come here to chill out and to leave the city behind."

Saratoga Inn
201 Cascade Avenue
Langley, WA 98260
(360) 221-5801
www.saratogainnwhidbeyisland.com

The Saratoga Inn features ramped access to the wraparound porch from the adjacent parking area.

Sleeping in Seattle

SEATTLE, WASHINGTON

*L*ocated in one of Seattle's most colorful neighborhoods, Pike Place Market attracts visitors and locals alike. This historic venue features over seven acres jam-packed with fish merchants, flower vendors, produce stands, musicians, artists, restaurants, and boutiques. It's truly a treat for the senses and a must-see when visiting the Emerald City. Of course, the best way to fully experience Pike Place Market is to stay nearby, and as luck would have it, two accessible choices are located within rolling distance.

The Inn at the Market is located in the center of Pike Place Market, on the corner of First Avenue and Pine Street. This 70-room luxury inn features an ivy-draped courtyard filled with charming shops, inviting restaurants, and a bubbling fountain. The inn first opened in 1985, and in 2002 four rooms were renovated to make them fully wheelchair-accessible.

Rooms 301, 302, 401 and 402 feature level thresholds, wide doorways, and good pathway access. Each accessible bathroom has a roll-in shower with a hand-held showerhead and a built-in shower seat, a roll-under sink, and grab bars in the shower and around the toilet. There is a full five-foot turning radius in the bathrooms and plenty of room to maneuver a wheelchair or scooter throughout the guest rooms.

There is barrier-free access to all of the inn's public areas. The third-floor rooms are accessible from street level, while the fourth-floor rooms are accessible by elevator. Valet parking and ramp access to the lobby are available at the Pine Street entrance. It's important to note that this is not the best pedestrian entrance as it's at the top of a very steep hill; however, the inn also has an alternate level pedestrian entrance.

Nightly rates for the accessible rooms range from $165 to $250.

It should also be noted that the Inn at the Market went above and beyond access requirements during their renovation, as a 70-room property is only required to have one room with a roll-in shower. In short, the management goes above and beyond in all areas, and they do whatever they can to

Room 12 at the Inn at Harbor Steps features a queen-sized bed and a very spacious sitting area.

make their guests comfortable. So don't be afraid to make special requests at this very accommodating establishment.

Two blocks up the street, next to Seattle's famous Harbor Steps, you'll find another accessible lodging choice, the Inn at Harbor Steps. Actually this 20-room inn is located at the base of one of Seattle's most elegant high-rise residential buildings. The inn rooms are on the garden level and they face the fountains of the Harbor Steps.

There is level access to the front entry of the building and barrier-free access throughout the lobby. Inn guests are directed to a separate registration area in the inner lobby, as the concierge desk in the outer lobby area serves the residential section of the building. As confusing as this may all seem at first, it's actually a very streamlined and efficient process.

Accessible parking is available in the building garage for $15 per night, and guests are directed to that area after registration. You can park out in front for a short time while registering, but during peak hours it may be difficult to find an open spot.

Room 12 is the accessible room, and it has a queen-sized bed, a fireplace, a wet bar, a refrigerator, and a coffeemaker. Access features include a level threshold, wide doorways, and good pathway access. The bathroom has a five-foot turning radius and a tub/shower combination with grab bars and a hand-held shower. There is also a roll-under sink and grab bars around the toilet. A shower chair is available upon request.

All of the public rooms are accessible at the Inn at Harbor Steps. A buffet breakfast is available every morning in the dining area, and afternoon hors d'oeuvres are served in the library. The accessible Wolfgang Puck restaurant is located in the building and provides room service to inn guests.

Nightly rates for the accessible room range from $165 to $180.

The Seattle Art Museum, which offers barrier-free access, is located right across the street from the Inn at Harbor Steps. And the waterfront area is only two blocks away and is accessible by a public elevator inside the inn.

Curb-cuts and sidewalks are ubiquitous in Seattle, but be prepared for some hills. That doesn't mean it's not accessible, it just means you have to plan your route carefully. An accessible map to downtown Seattle is available through King County Metro, and it's a must-have resource to fully explore this exciting city.

Inn at the Market
86 Pine Street
Seattle, WA 98101
(206) 443-3600
www.innatthemarket.com

Inn at Harbor Steps
1221 First Avenue
Seattle, WA 98101
(206) 748-0973
www.innatharborsteps.com

Feathered Star B&B

EGG HARBOR, WISCONSIN

*L*ocated halfway between Sturgeon Bay and Egg Harbor on Wisconsin's Door Peninsula, at first glance the Feathered Star B&B resembles a turn-of-the-century farmhouse; however, this newly constructed building was specifically designed with access in mind.

As a former occupational therapist, innkeeper Sandy Chlubna already had a good working knowledge of barrier-free design before she ever broke ground; although she readily admits she was fortunate to find an architect who was also familiar with the concept. She adds, "I also consulted a local organization involved in modifying and designing accessible buildings prior to starting construction." Her time and planning paid off, as today the Feathered Star houses a variety of accessible guest rooms.

All of the guest rooms feature wide doorways and good pathway access. The differences are in the bathrooms, bed types, and counter heights. Rooms 3 and 6 have roll-in showers, while the other four rooms have tub/shower combinations with fold-down shower seats. All bathrooms have grab bars, hand-held showers, and roll-under sinks. The countertops are of slightly varying heights, but as Sandy points out, "all are within ADA guidelines."

Rooms 2 and 6 each have two twin beds, while the other rooms have queen-sized beds. The beds are all different heights, and if an extra (or lower) bed is needed, Sandy has trundles available. Each room also has a small porch.

All the public areas of the Feathered Star are accessible, with wide doorways and minimal thresholds. The gently sloping sidewalk provides barrier-free access to the front porch and the house.

Nightly rates range from $100 to $130.

And don't worry, there's plenty to do in Door County, especially if you like the outdoors. During the summer many of the villages have festivals. There are also five state parks and numerous county and private sanctuaries with trails nearby. And as Sandy happily reports, "Tourism is a major industry here and people are becoming more aware of the need to provide accessibility to their businesses."

Feathered Star B&B
6202 Highway 42
Egg Harbor, WI 54209
(920) 743-4066
www.featheredstar.com

Welcome HOME

Welcome HOME is more than a B&B, it's a showplace for barrier-free design. The acronym in the name pretty much describes the property—HOME stands for House of Modification Examples. This universal design demonstration home is the brainchild of polio survivor and innkeeper Diane Miller.

For 30 years Diane relied on crutches to get around, but when the time came to transition to a wheelchair, she realized that some serious home modifications were also in order. In the beginning she thought it would be easy to find contractors and vendors that were well versed in universal design, but she soon learned that was not the case. "I thought I'd make a few calls, but the more calls I made, the more I realized that no one had any idea how to do this right," Diane explained.

So she hit the bricks and researched things on her own. In the end, she ended up not only with an accessible home, but also with a living reference library of sorts for others looking to make access modifications to their own homes. Ultimately, Diane's goal is to improve the quality of life for people living with physical disabilities. Says Diane, "By designing, building and maintaining a unique single-family home, we have created a vehicle for providing information, and examples of barrier-free living design."

Located 30 miles north of Milwaukee, Welcome HOME offers day visitors the opportunity to explore the entire home to gather ideas and determine which designs will work best for them. The B&B part of the business also allows overnight guests to give the equipment a real hands-on test.

Overnight guests are given free run of an entire wing of the house. The guest wing has a private entrance with covered accessible parking located next to the entrance, two accessible bedrooms, and two accessible bathrooms. Guests share a screened porch, the family room, and the kitchenette.

The Sara Room has a queen-sized bed plus a fold-out twin. The J.C. Penney Room offers a double bed, a twin waterbed and a fold-out futon. A Hoyer lift is available for either room. Located across the hall, one bathroom has a whirlpool tub with a door that swings open, and the other bathroom has a continental-style roll-in shower. Both bathrooms have grab bars in the bath and shower areas and around the toilets. Of course, the whole house features wide doorways, level thresholds, and excellent pathway access.

The nightly rate for the J.C. Penney Room or the Sara Room is $50. If you'd like a bit more privacy, you can rent the whole wing for $100 per night.

Surrounded by 17 acres of woodlands and accessible hiking trails, Welcome HOME is the perfect place to unwind. Diane is also very knowledgeable about accessible sights and attractions in the area. Say Diane, "We're very informal here. Come as you are, and bring a friend!"

Welcome HOME
4260 W. Hawthorne Drive
Newburg, WI 53060
(262) 675-2525
www.hnet.net/~welcomehome

Cheyenne Roundup

D escribed by many as a quintessential Wild West town, Cheyenne truly echoes the spirit of the Old West. Indeed, a visit to Cheyenne is like a trip back in time. Today the remnants of yesteryear linger in the well-preserved buildings and stately mansions of Cheyenne's historic district. And among those historic buildings are two nicely accessible B&Bs.

Located in the Rainsford historic district in lower downtown, the Rainsford Inn was the first B&B in Cheyenne. Built in 1903, it was once the home of Justice Van De Vanter, the only Wyoming judge to serve on the U.S. Supreme Court. Today this lovingly restored mansion is filled with antiques, and innkeepers Murray and Cindy Adams welcome guests to their unique six-room inn.

Murray and Cindy honeymooned at the Rainsford Inn, and during their stay they fell in love with Cheyenne. When the opportunity came to purchase the property, they jumped at it. Says Murray, "The access upgrades were already in place when we purchased the property, but I like the fact that we are able to offer wheelchair access. You just don't see that in a lot of historic properties."

The accessible Garden Room is located on the ground floor, just off of the dining room. It features wide doorways and good pathway access, and it is furnished with a queen-sized bed. The bathroom has a large roll-in shower with a built-in shower bench and a hand-held showerhead, a roll-under sink, lever handles, and grab bars in the shower and around the toilet.

There is barrier-free access to the entire ground floor, as the wide doorways make maneuvering very easy.

The rate for the Garden Room ranges from $60 to $67.50 per night.

Says Murray, "The inn kind of reminds guests of a visit to Grandma's house."

Located just one block away, the Nagle Warren Mansion was built in 1888. Innkeeper Jim Osterfoss purchased the property in 1997 and proceeded to renovate it. It was a lengthy process, and construction continued well into 2000.

Access was a concern to Jim during the renovation, but to be honest he sees access as just another amenity or customer-service issue. In the end he added an accessible guest room when he renovated the carriage house in 1999. "I had two access objectives with the carriage house renovation," says Jim. "I wanted to provide access to the first floor of the mansion, and I wanted to provide accessible guest accommodations that would match the mansion experience." After the dust settled, Jim had accomplished both of his objectives.

Today the accessible Marie Pershing Room is an excellent choice for wheelchair-users. There is level access to the carriage house from the parking area on House Avenue, and the Marie Pershing Room is located in the back of the carriage house. French doors open out to the garden and provide a lovely view of the herb garden.

The room features wide doorways, good pathway access, and a trapeze bracket over the bed. Access features in the bathroom include a roll-in shower with a hand-held showerhead, a roll-under sink, and grab bars in the shower and around the toilet. A toilet riser is available upon request.

The Marie Pershing Room at the Nagle Warren Mansion features an accessible bathroom with a roll-in shower. (Photo courtesy of the Nagle Warren Mansion.)

There is lift access from the carriage house connector to the first floor of the mansion. The first floor includes the dining room, parlor, library, and sitting room. From the connector you can also wheel out to the hot tub, the patio, and the yard.

The rate for the Marie Pershing Room ranges from $98 to $148 per night.

Jim points out that it's an easy and safe walk to many businesses and restaurants, the capitol building complex, and most state government offices. "The Whipple House Restaurant and Lexie's Mesa Grill are next door in historic homes and both are accessible," he adds. "And if you want to explore the outdoors, the Cheyenne Greenway is a twelve-mile recreational path that is fully accessible. We really have a lot of variety here in Cheyenne."

Rainsford Inn
219 East 18th Street
Cheyenne, WY 82001
(307) 638-2337
www.rainsfordinnbedandbreakfast.com

Nagle Warren Mansion
222 E. 17th Street
Cheyenne, WY 82001
(307) 637-3333
www.naglewarrenmansion.com

Index